A Jeweler's
GUIDE to
APPRENTICESHIPS

TABLE OF CONTENTS

- **6** How This Guide Can Be Used
- **8** Introduction by Charles Lewton-Brain

CHAPTER 1
- **12** Planning for an Apprentice

CHAPTER 2
- **26** Finding an Apprentice

CHAPTER 3
- **38** Training the Apprentice

CHAPTER 4
- **66** Training for Tool Identification
  - 68 Group One: Cutting Tools
  - 71 Group Two: Bending/Shaping Tools
  - 79 Group Three: Measuring/Marking Tools
  - 82 Group Four: Torch Tools

CHAPTER 5
- **86** Training for Safety
  - 88   Safety Rules for Jewelry Manufacturing
  - 89   General Safety Test
  - 90   Casting Equipment Safety Checkpoints
  - 93   Buffing Machine Safety Checkpoints
  - 94   Grinding Machine Safety Checkpoints
  - 97   Buffing Machine/Grinding Wheel Safety Test
  - 99   Drill Press Safety Checkpoints
  - 102 Drill Press Safety Test
  - 104 Hydraulic Press Safety Checkpoints

107	Hydraulic Press Safety Test
108	Laser Equipment Safety Checkpoints
110	Safe Torch Procedures
116	Torch Work Safety Test
118	Test Answer Keys

CHAPTER 6
124 Training for Skill

125	Basic Soldering: Practice Exercises
128	Creating Filed Cuff Bracelets
138	Wax Carving
148	Rivet Capture Pendant
160	Slot-in-Slot Construction
174	Introductory Filigree Bead

CHAPTER 7
188 Advice for Those Beginning Their Jewelry Careers

201 Addendum: A Jeweler's Vocabulary

206 Index

208 About the Author & Consulting Editor

Apprenticeship Success Stories

32	Jo G. Haemer	120	Amber Worley
35	Timothy Green	182	Sam Patania
60	G. Phil Poirier	185	Ronda Coryell
63	Maria Samora	196	Nanz Aalund

© 2017 MJSA
ISBN 978-0-9799962-3-8
Library of Congress Control Number: 2017913510

All rights reserved. No part of this book may be reproduced in any form or by any electronic or mechanical means, including information storage and retrieval systems, without permission in writing from the copyright holders, except for brief passages quoted in review.

Published by MJSA, 8 Hayward St., Attleboro, MA 02703; 1-800-444-MJSA (6572) or 1-401-274-3840; e-mail *info@mjsa.org*; *MJSA.org*.

Cover image by Jessica Endresen. Apprentice: Kyle Cetnarowski. Cover master goldsmith: Jane Corey.

The images on the following pages were provided by Rio Grande (*riogrande.com*): 66, 68-83, 91, 95 (buffing machine), 105, 111, 160, 174. The image of the grinding machine on page 95 is courtesy of Wen Products (*wenproducts.com*). Additional photos are courtesy of Ronda Coryell (185-87), Gary Dawson (22, 50), Jessica Endresen (12), Timothy Green (35–37), Jo Haemer (32, 34, 52), Sam Patania (128, 132-37, 182-83), G. Phil Poirier (60, 62), Maria Samora (63–65), Amber Worley (120, 122–23). Images on the following pages were supplied by iStockphoto.com artists (in parentheses): 17 (Razvan), 21 (minimero), 26 (Razvan), 47 (eyenigelen), 48 (Homonstock), 86 (King Wu), 93 (alexandrayurkina), 101 (luril Garmash), and 188 (miljko). All other images are courtesy of the author (photographer: Doug Yaple).

A Jeweler's Guide to Apprenticeships is part of the
MJSA BEaJEWELER program (*beajeweler.com*), which is
funded in part by a grant from the JCK Industry Fund.

Safety Notice: The contents of this book have not been tested or authorized by MJSA. The use or application of information, practices, and/or techniques pertaining to jewelry making, jewelry repair, or other related topics in this book may be hazardous to persons and property, and they are undertaken at the reader's own risk. Please use all appropriate safety measures.

For Prof. Mary Lee Hu

HOW THIS GUIDE CAN BE USED BY...

Professional Shop Owners

This guide will enable you to more easily institute an apprenticeship program in your shop. It will help you to plan for it, to select an apprentice who is passionate and motivated, and to train that apprentice through the use of exercises that teach fundamental knowledge and specific skills, with an emphasis on safety.

Apprentices

By reading this guide's chapters, you will have a better understanding of the jewelry business owner's goals and challenges in taking you on. It will also help you to learn what your potential employer needs from you and how you can best facilitate that learning. Even if you plan on starting your own jewelry business, your best opportunity to learn how that is done is by working for a successful company first.

Self-Directed Learners

Use the learning objectives and goals to establish and measure your own progress. Read the success stories of how others got into the jewelry business and see if their experiences can inspire your own path. Seek out mentors in your part of the country and travel to workshops given by master craftsmen you admire. No matter what your level of training currently is, take the time to review the safety portion of this guide. Familiarize yourself and test yourself with the safety standards tests. Go online and study safety and operational standards for various jewelry equipment, and the Safety Data Sheets for compounds and chemicals used in jewelry processes.

Students

If you are currently in a jewelry/metals program, take ownership of your education. Talk with your professors and engage them with the career path you hope to take. Seek out the best training from established jewelry-making masters. Push yourself to gain greater competency in traditional metalsmithing techniques and seek classes in a broad range of illustrative and 3-D software, as well as business and marketing classes.

Instructors

If you are a high school teacher or college instructor in metal arts, use this book to help you structure your syllabus. Encourage your students to practice skills that will help them become employable in the jewelry trade. Use the safety tests and practice projects as part of your curriculum. Reach out to local businesses and cooperate to build community support for your programs.

Introduction

Today's American jewelry world is a changing one. The number of independent jewelry retailers in North America has decreased significantly over the past decade—between 2015 and 2016 alone, the Jewelers Board of Trade recorded a drop of 1,230 retailers, a 5.5 percent decline. Analysts have pointed to various causes, from owner retirements to increasing competition from online sellers. On the other hand, technology—in the form of computer-assisted jewelry design and manufacturing (CAD/CAM)—has aided both manufacturers and retailers, particularly in the dynamic area of custom design.

But CAD/CAM work still needs great design and planning, as well as old-fashioned skill in metal casting, gem setting, and finishing. Whether you use digital technologies or old-world techniques, jewelry-making remains a center of high-end hand skills and quality craftsmanship that's still greatly valued. But getting quality skills in an employee can be difficult, as many in the industry can attest. I have heard numerous stories of jewelers repeatedly flying people in to test who didn't work out. Part of the problem is that, while there are some technical schools that do a good job of educating potential bench jewelers, the majority of jewelry-making programs can be found in art colleges. And while these colleges do provide some good problem-solving skills, I have found they often do not have the time or resources to take their students to the technical level required by many professional jewelers.

One answer is to train your own goldsmiths though apprenticeship programs. Organized apprenticeships have been generally absent from America since the late 1970s and early '80s, thanks largely to the decline of jewelers' unions (including the International Jewelry Workers Union) that promoted the apprentice/journeyman structure. However, apprenticeships still offer many benefits: They can ultimately raise the quality work in your shop, expand your staff with workers who are committed to you and your business, and keep jewelry traditions and long-term client relationships strong. And they can still be found, as some jewelers have developed individual programs (often based on their own European training). Their approach is similar to the one you'll find in the book you're now holding.

Written by Nanz Aalund, a committed educator as well as a talented jewelry artist and designer, this readable book will enable you to more easily institute an apprenticeship in your own shop, regardless of your background. It will show you how to plan for an apprenticeship; how to evaluate and choose a candidate who is passionate and motivated; and how to train that person to work both *for* you and *with* you. It also includes projects and exercises that teach specific skills, with safety emphasized throughout. In addition, the book is designed not only to provide support as you take on an apprentice, but also to help the apprentice understand what is required to take advantage of the opportunity. It is a tool for both of you.

Obviously, the benefits of quality work, committed workers, and better client relationships are compelling reasons for instituting an apprenticeship. Depending on your location, there may even be city/government/service organizations or foundations to help subsidize the apprenticeship position. However, some jewelers might be concerned that apprentices will take their new skills to a competitor, or that the learning curve will lead to slower production rates, which could then affect the bottom line. If you share such concerns, consider this:

• Many workplace studies show that apprentices are, in general, loyal. One study by the Canadian Apprenticeship Forum (*caf-fca.org*) found that "apprentices felt more loyalty to employers who supported and eventually hired them."

• The Canadian Apprenticeship Forum also demonstrated a proven return of $1.47 for every $1 invested in apprenticeship training. A study by the Economics & Statistics Administration of the U.S. Department of Commerce found similar returns.

For the right apprentice, this path is a life choice. And for the right employer, an apprenticeship is an investment in the future—the apprentice's, their business's, the industry's. Apprenticeships are, in short, vital—and, hopefully, this book will help the apprenticeship model to regain its stature as a link to a successful career.

There has been nothing like this book published in America before, and I commend Nanz and MJSA highly for this endeavor. If it increases the number and quality of available apprenticeships and training opportunities, it will have done its work—and made a big difference to the field of professional jewelry making and design.

Charles Lewton-Brain
Associate Professor, Jewellery and Metals Program
Alberta College of Art & Design
Calgary, Alberta, Canada
May 2017

CHAPTER 1

FOR AN APPRENTICE

One of the first questions I am asked when I talk to jewelry business owners about hiring an apprentice is: What happens if an apprentice breaks an expensive piece of my customer's jewelry? And my response is always the same: An apprentice should handle a customer's jewelry item only to transport it, for no other reason. Then comes the question, "Well, what good are they then?" Remarkably, the logic jumps from "I can't hire an apprentice because they will cause irreparable damage" to "They will be useless." In reality, with some advance planning and a widened perspective, neither of these alternatives needs to be true.

The Advantages of an Apprenticeship Program

Apprenticeships are a wonderful way for students in the jewelry field to gain experience, but they are also useful for your business. Among the benefits:

- New, creative individuals will help you to gain fresh insights into your existing practices, get exposure to new ideas, and rally enthusiasm for higher craftsmanship.

• An apprenticeship program can help you to better recruit well-suited staff, especially for small to mid-sized companies. When you "try out" a candidate during a semester or summer apprenticeship, you avoid the pitfalls of taking on a new hire only to find out that the person is not a good fit for your organization, or doesn't like the segment of the jewelry field in which your company is engaged. An apprenticeship program allows you to benefit from added workforce help while being able to more accurately assess potential full-time employees.

• The added help of an apprenticeship also enables your business to take advantage of short-term support for special projects. With training, an apprentice's extra set of hands will help your skilled employees to be more productive, freeing them up to accomplish more creative tasks that require their higher-level strategic thinking and expertise.

• The intentional promotion of your apprenticeship program—through your local chamber of commerce or local press—can enhance community loyalty for your business. If you offer an impressive apprenticeship program with a notable apprentice supervisor/mentor, your apprentices will talk about their experiences with peers, social media "friends," and family members, essentially advertising your business and its services for free.

Steps to Take Prior to Initiating an Apprenticeship Program

While a worthwhile apprenticeship experience can and should be mutually beneficial, you first must lay the groundwork. The following outline can help you to ensure that both your shop and the apprentice will gain the maximum reward from the program.

1. Involve all current employees by discussing apprentice-related issues at staff meetings or during one-on-ones with the managers. Without big-picture buy-in and staff cooperation, an apprentice will not feel welcome, focused, or engaged. And conflicting directives from uninformed staff members may make it difficult for an apprentice to meet specific program goals.

2. Conduct an informal survey of your employees. Some sample questions to ask:

What tasks and special projects require attention? What skill sets could your shop benefit from? Could any workflow areas and organizational tasks in the manufacturing shop or office be eased with additional help?

3. Based on that survey, make a list of the tasks and projects to which an apprentice could be assigned, and which skills would be needed.

4. Determine who could best serve as workplace supervisor, and see if their duties could be revised so that they have the time and resources not only to effectively train and manage the apprentice, but also to manage the program itself. Involve additional staff members by assigning them key roles in specific training areas, so the program can run more smoothly.

5. Decide when the apprenticeship should take place (steer clear of the stressful holiday season) and the amount of time that would be best to host an apprentice. (See Chapter 3, pages 41-42, for an overview of the most common apprenticeship timeframes.) To facilitate proper planning, you should elect a launch date of at least 8 to 10 weeks out—if you selected a summer timeframe, for instance, initiate the program planning, candidate search, and hiring process in March.

6. Figure out how to arrange the physical space of your business to accommodate an additional individual. (Ideally, the apprentice's bench would be next to—or in close proximity to—the workplace supervisor.)

7. Make sure your shop has basic security precautions in place, including video monitoring, alarm systems, safes, and established security practices for staff. To minimize liability risks, you should maintain standardized health and safety procedures, provide Safety Data Sheet (SDS) information, and comply with Occupational Safety and Health Administration (OSHA) regulations.

8. Research the legal ramifications of hosting an apprentice in your state. Consult with the Small Business Administration (*sba.gov*) or your state's labor department for information on employment and labor law, including which full-time employee benefits apply to an apprentice. Look into the regulations regarding workers' compensation, safety and harassment policies, age restrictions, and wage requirements. Speak with your company's human resource manager or legal counsel, or consult with an employment law professional through your local chamber of commerce.

9. Talk with your accountant and draw up a possible budget to determine whether your company can support one or more apprentices, and the financial impact it might have.

10. Develop a structure for the program. (In Chapter 3, you'll find how to accomplish this aspect.) Using the key information offered in this guide while adding your company's behavioral expectations, security protocol, and daily duties, you can ensure that the structure of your apprenticeship program will suit your company's unique needs.

Based on staff input, make a list of tasks and projects for the apprentice, and which skills will be needed.

Compensating the Apprentice

The logic of past eras, when apprentices were unpaid laborers or indentured servants who exchanged their time and labor for the educational experience of learning a trade, no longer holds up. Establishing an apprenticeship program as a means of receiving free labor violates the Fair Labor Standards Act (FLSA), which states that "the employer that provides the training derives no immediate advantage from the activities of the trainees, and on occasion the employer's operations may actually be impeded." The impediments your company may incur can be as slight as the time it takes to organize and implement an apprenticeship program, yet it is important to take the FLSA into consideration.

With an apprenticeship, you are legally obligated to offer at least minimum wage. The Code of Federal Regulations, Title 29, Chapter 1, part 29.5, states that you must provide:

A progressively increasing schedule of wages to be paid the apprentice consistent with the skill acquired. The entry wage shall be not less than the minimum wage prescribed by the Fair Labor Standards Act, where applicable, unless a higher wage is required by other applicable Federal law, State law, respective regulations, or by collective bargaining agreement.

To establish a baseline wage to offer, research current trends and applicant expectations of acceptable compensation. For a gauge of a "going rate," check what a local temp agency is paying its temp workers. This rate is often slightly higher than the minimum wage in order to attract higher-qualified candidates. You are not obligated to pay unemployment, offer health insurance, or provide a severance package should you choose not to hire the person at the end of the apprenticeship. If you do wish to hire the apprentice permanently, you'll need to reevaluate the compensation rate. Fair and adequate pay is the number-one reason companies retain employees.

Can the Apprenticeship Earn College Credits?

While an apprenticeship is definitely a "learning" experience, whether or not it qualifies for educational credits must be arranged with each school where said credits could be obtained. It is a misconception that apprenticeship work can be easily and equally exchanged for college or university credits. In reality, established collaborative programs between the jewelry industry and most educational institutions no longer exist. It is up to the candidate to pursue credit for an apprenticeship with their educational institution; your company cannot offer college credits directly as part of compensation unless you have established a program that has been accepted by an educational facility.

As an alternative to a paid apprenticeship, you can try to establish an internship program in conjunction with a local university or college metals program. This requires effort on the part of the business owner to cultivate and maintain the cooperation of the educational institution, and you may also need to have someone on staff with teaching experience or an advanced degree. Once established, though, an internship could provide a steady stream of apprentices who will come to you with some metalsmithing experience. (Read "Advice on Establishing a Joint Training Program," page 22, to see how goldsmith/designer Gary Dawson set up an internship program with the University of Oregon.) Further on, this guide will offer additional structure and adult educational techniques to ensure that an apprenticeship or internship, depending on which you decide to pursue, will not end up badly.

Plan for What Happens *After* the Apprenticeship

An apprenticeship is a great way to assess the potential of a student, recent grad, or possible new hire, allowing you to gauge their skill levels and work ethic during this trial period. While it is important to give the apprentice real, meaningful work that will help your company accomplish more, run smoother, and complete projects more efficiently, there is the concern about what happens after the apprenticeship is over. What if the now-former apprentice is seeking employment with a competitor, possibly taking your proprietary designs with them? If this is a concern for your business, a "non-compete agreement" should be devised with the help of a legal service and signed by apprentice candidates before beginning their apprenticeships. A non-compete agreement should be limited to design ideas generated at your firm; it should not limit the apprentice's ability to find work within any specific geographic location. Any restriction that creates an undue burden on the apprentice's efforts to make a living may make the agreement unenforceable. Another way to address this concern is to make sure the apprenticeship program focuses on projects that support your craftspeople in ways that are not directly involved with your business's proprietary design work.

The best way to minimize risks to your business is to start with a solid understanding of the process and to establish a flexible, well-established apprenticeship plan that can be adapted to your unique business needs. Once you create it, initiating an apprenticeship program can be as easy as checking items off a list.

With training, an apprentice's extra set of hands will help your skilled employees be more productive.

Advice on Establishing an Internship Program

Gary Dawson, a goldsmith and custom jeweler who currently operates Gary Dawson Designs in Eugene, Oregon, has long been an advocate of preparing students for professional careers. Below he describes how he worked with the University of Oregon to develop an internship program at his then-business, Goldworks.

Please tell me how and why your jewelry business established a program for students.

GD: Metals students who discover they love the medium and then decide to pursue careers in jewelry or metalworking may encounter difficulties. Matriculating from the highly conceptual work of academia into a more structured world of metal-as-a-means-of-support may be made more difficult by the occasional lack of communication and cooperation between these two outlooks. It was this difficulty that we addressed in the establishment of a permanent working internship program with the University of Oregon Jewelry and Metalsmithing department. Closely related to the concept of an apprentice yet different, an intern is by definition "an advanced student or a recent graduate undergoing supervised practical training."

How did you find the students?

My shop had already been "discovered" by some of the metal art students from the University of Oregon Jewelry and Metalsmithing department. I think that the relevance to students of this program is underscored by the fact that the original idea [for an internship program] was brought to me by a student. In 1998, an outgoing employee introduced me to a student who suggested he could work for credits. The idea intrigued me, as I realized that I had a variety of things I could offer students besides a paid position. I had 10 years of teaching experience through the U. of O. Craft Center and private workshops, and my shop could offer training in the practical application of goldsmithing techniques with three working journeyman goldsmiths in the studio.

How did you structure this program?

The program started out in a very loosely organized manner in the summer of 1998, and after some discussion with Kate Wagle, the head of the Jewelry and Metalsmithing department at the time, we initiated the pilot program with one student. We felt the program would work best for both students and my shop if students participated for two consecutive terms (approximately eight months) with a minimum time commitment of 12 to 16 hours per week. This schedule was equivalent to a three- to four-credit course per term. In my proposal, I asked that students be prepared to participate in all shop activities, from cleaning duties to actual goldsmithing to working the sales floor. Students would submit portfolios, resumés, and statements for me to consider.

In 2003, Kate Wagle, Tracy Steepy—a metals instructor at U. of O.—my shop manager, and I finalized the following format.

Internship Criteria

1. Candidate must be a University of Oregon student in good standing (3.0 GPA or better) currently enrolled in a BFA or graduate art degree program with intermediate to advanced metalworking skills.

2. Candidate must submit (1) an application form, (2) a resumé, (3) one letter of recommendation, (4) a personal statement indicating how the internship would benefit them, specifying the particular area(s) of interest, and (5) five slides of completed metal projects.

3. Candidate should be willing and able to participate for a minimum of two terms of three to four credit hours each. Credit hours will be earned at the ratio of one credit hour for every four hours of work in the Goldworks studio per week.

4. Application materials (#2 above) should be submitted to Jewelry and Metalsmithing faculty for review and forwarded to Gary Dawson at least three weeks prior to the end of a term for the following term.

Internship Requirements/Expectations:

1. Honesty and integrity in the shop at all times.
2. Commitment and timeliness regarding work schedule.
3. Neatness of appearance. (We are a retail environment.)
4. Cheerful participation in any shop-related activity, including but not necessarily limited to: cleaning and maintenance of shop and tools, answering phone in a professional manner, greeting

and servicing retail clients, setup and takedown, assisting in line production, all phases of bench work, and office duties.

5. A journal about the internship must be kept, and a 20-minute class presentation needs to be delivered (with support from Gary Dawson and faculty).

6. Design and completion of one precious-metal project (usually involving one or more gems) suitable for display and sale.

7. Completion of feedback form at end of term.

What benefits do you feel a company could gain from this program?

I sincerely believe that, under the best of circumstances, the choice to train can be a fantastic investment in a company's financial future and competitiveness. But like responding to a personal ad, it could also be (at the very least) a temporary disaster if one were to blunder into the situation without some forethought and preparation.

CHAPTER 2

Finding
AN APPRENTICE

Searching for a great apprentice is similar to initiating an apprenticeship program: both require diligent planning. In this chapter, you'll find recruiting tips to make your search easier.

To find the right candidate, it is extremely helpful to have a clear idea of what your expectations are and to communicate that in a position profile. Before you post the position, consider drafting an apprentice profile. Review the list of tasks, projects, and necessary skills you created in Chapter 1; these will provide some clear directives for the profile and a job description. While this written profile of an "ideal apprentice" may be wishful thinking, it can at least act as a model for your ad and ultimately may help to narrow down the candidates.

Searching for the Apprentice

Once your ad is ready, the next question is where to post it. Rather than relying on large online classified sites, such as Craigslist (which may expose your business to bogus applicants and theft risk), try connecting with grassroots networks in your community. Send out a press release promoting your apprenticeship program as a human interest story. Include information about your apprentice search in your social media feeds and e-newsletters (which will not only draw potential leads, but also tell your customers that they're helping to provide meaningful job training by patronizing your business). Promote the position through your local Chamber of Commerce (*uschamber.com*) or Rotary (*rotary.org*), which will show other local business leaders that you are engaged in helping youth in your community.

Since jewelry job searches are traditionally communicated by word of mouth, contacting jewelry-related organizations can help you to broaden your search while at the same time targeting candidates already in the jewelry field. Some organizations, such as the Women's Jewelry Association (WJA) and the Gemological Institute of America (GIA) Alumni Association, may have local chapters through which you can spread the word. In this same vein, regional metal arts groups have members that already possess some basic jewelry-making skills. Often these groups (or guilds) have newsletters where an article about your apprenticeship search would reach an interested audience. All of these organizations have monthly meetings or social events, through which you can broaden your business's grassroots community network.

The MJSA BEaJEWELER program (*beajeweler.com*) offers another opportunity to find candidates. Although this is a national program, it is often visited by prospective jewelers seeking internships and apprenticeships. Not only can the BEaJEWELER website and social media outlets promote your opportunity, but the program's parent association, MJSA (*MJSA.org*), can assist in helping to find suitable candidates.

You can also join Ganoksin (*ganoksin.com*), an informational resource for jewelry makers, and post your opportunity to its Orchid online forum (which runs daily threads about jewelry-making issues and opportunities).

Finally, don't forget about local schools. Try reaching out to high school art teachers as well as community college and university metal arts programs; they may be helpful in recommending candidates. They may also be able to suggest other resources. To find my first apprentice, I wrote to seven regional high school art teachers, and a couple of them directed me to contact a local city's government youth service program. Such programs offer another good resource, especially since they vet the students and pay a percentage of the apprentice's hourly wage.

Interviewing Candidates

Once you find suitable candidates, you'll need to assess them and determine which one best meets your position's requirements. Having a staff member participate in the interview can help a small business find an apprentice who will be a good fit within the company culture. Candidates may relax if the business owner leaves the room, giving an existing employee the opportunity to get a different perspective on the applicant's personality. Staff members, especially those who will be supervising the program, need to know if they will be able to work well on a day-to-day basis with a new apprentice and will appreciate being included in the interview process.

In addition to character traits such as honesty, integrity, and commitment, the successful candidate should have two important skill sets: problem solving and manual dexterity. To determine an individual's problem-solving ability, employ the **Behavioral Based Interviewing (BBI)** technique, a style of questioning designed to probe into a candidate's analytical aptitude.

The BBI questions require a three-part answer: Rather than asking questions that lead to a yes or no response, they require descriptive answers. Instead of asking the candidates what they have done, the questions focus on the ways they accomplished their goals and the reasons for their undertaking of these actions. Using the BBI strategy, you might first ask a candidate, "Explain a time when you came up with a simple solution for a complex problem," then follow up with, "How did you accomplish it and what was the outcome?" This technique will give you some concrete insight into the applicant's problem-solving abilities.

Another example would be to ask a candidate for an example of a situation that required a quick analysis of a difficult problem. Follow up with, "Were you able to find a solution?" and conclude by asking "How did that work out?" Developing other lead-ins, such as, "Can you give me a specific example of when…," "Tell me about a recent challenge that you…," or "Please describe a situation in which you were able to…" will allow you to use the time-tested BBI evaluation technique.

To test for a baseline of **manual dexterity**, you can purchase grooved pegboards and hand-tool dexterity test kits on the internet. These test kits, ranging from $100 to $250, have been designed to accurately measure and score the speed of an individual's eye/hand coordination and finger agility. Some tests ask the taker to assemble small parts with their fingers alone, while others require the use of tweezers or hand tools to complete assembly within a limited timeframe. The business owner can rank the candidates based on their test scores.

Implementing a manual dexterity test may be helpful in culling unsuitable candidates, as long as you remember that the fine motor skills required for jewelry making are learned skills, which usually increase in accuracy and speed with training and practice.

Tasks to Perform After the Interview

In closing, run a thorough online background check and call the references provided by the final candidate. After all, any individual who is coming into your business must be trustworthy.

Before contacting a reference, create a standard set of questions that focus on what the position will require of the applicant. Possible questions include:

- How well do you know the applicant?
- What are their strengths/weaknesses?
- Would you consider them trustworthy?
- What was their attendance record? Were they punctual?
- Would you consider them a hard worker? A problem solver? A quick learner?

Check at least three references. If you're interviewing a young person still in school, you can accept references from neighbors, teachers, or coaches, especially if this is the applicant's first work experience. When interviewing a candidate with hobby-level experience or from a college-level metals program, ask for work samples and have your shop foreman or a supervising goldsmith inspect them.

Apprenticeship SUCCESS STORY

JO G. HAEMER
Owner, Timothy W. Green, Portland, Oregon

How old were you when you started making jewelry/metals?
I was 17 years old when I started to work with metals, but I was unable to get into a union jewelry job straight out of school because of my gender. So I worked as a self-employed liturgical silversmith. I also worked retail until I could talk my way into a union shop.

How old were you when you started an apprenticeship?
I was 28 years old when I got hired at a union jewelry manufacturing shop. As a union member I was guaranteed a raise at least once a year until I reached journeyman's wages.

Did the apprenticeship have a structure? Was the structure shared with you?
Not really. I got an entry-level job as a polisher, floor sweeper, etc. I would just show up to work and do whatever they wanted me to. It was mostly work that none of the guys wanted to do, and that went on for five years.

Was there a jewelers' union you had to join to participate in the apprenticeship?
Yes, International Jewelry Workers Local 49.

Were you paired with a master craftsman to apprentice with?
As I transitioned from polisher to bench worker, I was placed at a bench next to one of the guys in the shop who showed me how to do repairs—tasks that a general repair person would need to perform. I was told that I was not allowed to learn stone setting because "women would break the gemstones during their periods." Hard to believe, isn't it?

In what techniques did you seek training?
I was first inspired by the idea of making my own eyeglasses when I met Deb Stoner, a studio jewelry artist. She worked as an eyeglass designer. Even though she was pretty much done making glasses when I met her, she was such a great help to me. She walked me through the basics of how to make the half-bezel eye wires that hold the lens, and how to cut a non-prescription lens. She was so very kind to share her

knowledge with me. She is a wonderful artist as well as a great teacher.

Several years ago, at the Portland Jewelery Symposium [held each fall in Portland, Oregon], Stuller representatives showed up with a new silver alloy called Continuum. It turned out to be the perfect alloy for my eyeglass designs. I asked John Butler and Shan Aithal, the metallurgists at Stuller, for more information. Their advice helped me to get off and running with the ideas I had.

Have you taken on an apprentice? Why/why not?

Tim Green and I have been in business together since 1991. We make only a handful of very high-end pieces a month. We have trained and taught a number of folks privately in our studio. We teach both experienced professionals as well as a few newbies. We usually take on only one or two folks a year. Most of the newbies have gone on to have careers in the trade. Although we have had several really great trainees, the one we still keep in touch with is Allison Daggett. She is a very high functioning Asperger's person. Her amazing imagination and absolute focus, as well as her dedication to excellence and raw talent, allowed us to help her move from working in a very low-paying "shelter" workshop to a career in the jewelry trade. Allison is our pride and joy.

Apprenticeship SUCCESS STORY

TIMOTHY GREEN
Owner, Timothy W. Green, Portland, Oregon

How old were you when you started making jewelry/metals?
I had jewelry classes starting in my third year of high school, and my father owned a sheet metal shop where I worked throughout high school.

What kind of training did you receive or seek?
I served a five-year apprenticeship at Zell Bros. Jewelers in Portland,

Oregon. It was a union shop, one of those jewelry shops inside a retail store with a window for the public to watch the craftsmen from [the showroom floor]. My uncle had worked there as a goldsmith for 42 years. [Zell Bros. closed in 2009 after 97 years in business.]

I was in the union from the start—the International Jewelry Workers Local 49—and stayed for 12 years. I was guaranteed a raise every six months for five years, at which time I was given a journeyman's pay and title. All of our files, burs, drill bits, and expendable shop supplies, including shop coats, were provided. I had no financial obligations other than buying special, personal hand tools I wanted.

Did you seek a master craftsman to apprentice with?

I apprenticed with a shop full of masters, including a diamond setter who was a World War II Marine [and] a model-and-mold maker who was a World War II Holocaust survivor, sitting next to a former Hitler youth, [who was] a master platinumsmith. There were journeymen fabricators, polishers, bench jewelers for repair, and hand engravers—all men, the youngest one in his mid-50s.

In which techniques were you trained?

I was encouraged to be an all-around jeweler and given design jobs very early on. I learned the business from the owners and by the seat of my pants. The store owners gladly paid for outside classes as well. I soaked up everything I could, and still love that I learn something new every day.

Have you taken on an apprentice? Why or why not?

About 25 years ago, Jo Haemer and I set up our shop in our home. We have never hired an official "apprentice," but we have hired other journeymen jewelers as independent subcontractors, and we have trained a fair share of jewelers too. We're lucky in that we take referrals only from other jewelers in the trade, so our students are very carefully vetted.

We train only folks who are serious about learning and using the skills we teach. By the time we get someone in our studio, the person is very dedicated to the chosen career path. We also get students from other jewelry manufacturers who want us to train their employees in advanced old-world skills. It is rewarding to know that old-world skills are still appreciated and sought after.

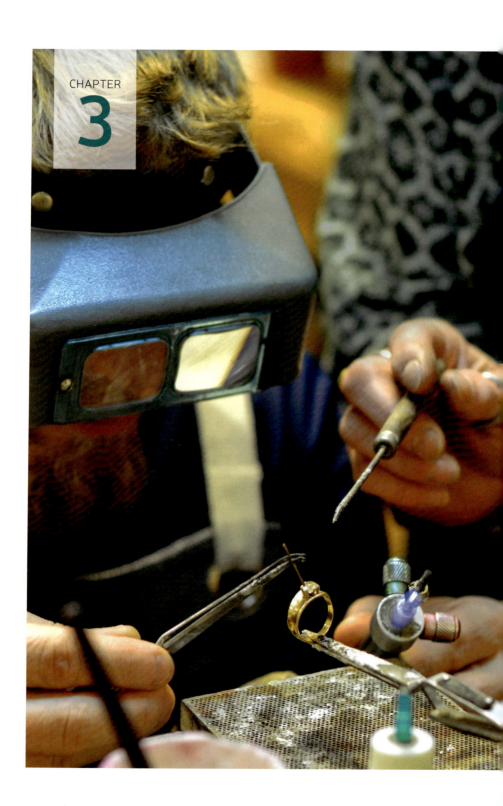

Training
THE APPRENTICE

Historically, apprentices were given jobs that supported the master craftspeople in accomplishing work on customers' jewelry. The apprentice would clean work areas and prepare raw materials, as well as maintain tools and equipment—work that, if performed by a higher-paid master goldsmith, would create a drag on shop productivity. Compared to custom work, such duties as casting ingots and rolling out sizing stock, drawing down wire, and making jump-rings are relatively low risk. Yet an apprentice's takeover of them would free up the master craftsperson to be more productive.

Apprentices were also trained in tasks that would lead to an understanding of the physical properties of the precious metals they would be expected to work with in their careers. Often, this was done with non-precious metals—the working properties of copper, for example, closely mirror those of sterling silver, just as the properties of brass resemble those of karat gold.

In this chapter, you'll find guidance on how to identify suitable tasks for an apprentice, determine the appropriate length of time for the apprenticeship, and implement a program that ensures the apprentice can achieve measurable goals and objectives.

Identifying Suitable Tasks

In Chapter 1, you drew up a list of projects and areas of need, which your staff identified. Here is where you will refer to that list and use it to develop a unique apprenticeship plan. If your company does in-house casting, an apprentice could perform "classic support tasks": inject, sprue, and invest waxes, as well as clean up the raw castings. If you are concerned with the risk of losing precious metals while training an unskilled person, have the apprentice run the training process with bronze first.

Other typical support tasks include:
- Cleaning the ultrasonic machine, as well as cleaning jewelry in the ultrasonic
- Flushing and maintaining the steam cleaner
- Pulling waxes for stock
- Tagging finished jewelry for display
- Sorting findings
- Cleaning and maintaining 3-D printers or CNC mills
- Cleaning and maintaining lasers or TIG welders
- Setting up and organizing digital design files
- Updating master model/mold catalogues
- Taking inventory of manufacturing expendables
- Digitally photographing finished jewelry for look books and social media

An upper-level (journeyman) craftsperson/staff member will need to organize and monitor these tasks, which can be combined with more traditional bench-skills training.

How Long Should an Apprenticeship Last?

The European model of apprenticeship calls for training to last five to seven years. Depending on the background and previous training of your apprentice candidate, as well as on the technical proficiency you're seeking, modified apprenticeship training—devised using this guide—could last anywhere from 90 days to two years.

The 90-day Apprenticeship Model

A 90-day probationary period is a well-established protocol for new hires. The 90-day apprenticeship model will provide the structure the business owner needs to assess an apprentice's skill and determine whether or not the person is a good fit. It is important to establish clear objectives an apprentice should accomplish within the 90 days. Depending on the educational level of the apprentice candidate, establishing three to four clearly delineated learning objectives is best. For example, a jewelry/metals graduate from a 2- or 4-year college or trade school could complete the safety tests provided in (Chapter 5) within the first week as one of the learning objectives.

This model works equally well for the summer employment of a college or high school student. However, employment laws in many states forbid the exposure of individuals under 18 to toxic chemicals, acids, and some industrial equipment. While these laws could limit the tasks a shop foreman or workplace supervisor could assign a 16- to an 18-year-old, this student could still fulfill numerous other tasks. Although a single summer would not be considered a true apprenticeship, a great deal of skill can be built by continued apprenticeship training through subsequent summers.

The Six-Month Apprenticeship Model:

If you are hiring an apprentice who does have a college-level jewelry program degree or perhaps is an advanced-level hobbyist jewelry maker, a six-month apprenticeship may adapt the person's skill set to acceptable levels for specific tasks. For a six-month model, you should set five to seven learning objectives in the skill sets your company will require. While limited in scope, this model will determine if the apprentice has the capacity to undertake additional training in a broader range of skills. It will also help you to discover whether this individual would be content working within the targeted niche your company's jewelry manufacturing process needs.

The Two-Year Apprenticeship:

With a two-year apprenticeship, you should devise five to seven new learning objectives every six months to ensure that the apprentice is gaining competency in a broad range of skills. Such a program should include additional training outside of your business; the options include a community college metals or CAD/CAM program, weekend-long regional metals guild workshops, or weeklong trade school intensives on specific skill sets. Providing tuition and travel benefits to the apprentice in exchange for a non-compete agreement or an extended employment commitment would be appropriate. By doing so, you ensure that the apprentice's new skill sets not only remain in-house, but also will be available for training future apprentices. However, if your business cannot or is not willing to make the financial commitment necessary for advanced training, you should not expect the apprentice to remain with your company if the apprentice has obtained additional advanced training without your assistance.

Writing Learning Objectives

Regardless of the candidate's background or the duration of the program you have selected, the success of an apprenticeship hinges on establishing clear learning objectives. To assess an apprentice's strengths or identify gaps in knowledge, you'll need to create assessable objectives and review them with the apprentice. Creating learning objectives with incremental goals will provide you both with tangible ways to measure progress. For example, the learning objectives for metals graduates from a college or trade school can be designed to assess the graduates' competency at fine soldering procedures—they may be adept at silver, for example, but not proficient in gold. For a less experienced apprentice, gaining competency in more elemental procedures, such as safe handling of a torch and the proper use of a rolling mill, will be more appropriate.

To establish clear objectives for an apprentice, you will need to determine what you are going to ask the apprentice to do before the person reports for work. Again, refer to your list from Chapter 1. Consider which tasks from that list the apprentice would be able to work on alone with minimal training and which tasks should be addressed as a team. Define the tasks the apprentice will be able to do independently by the end of the apprenticeship. Each item in which the apprentice will gain competency is an objective. Depending on the length of the apprenticeship, identify three to seven objectives and write out the incremental goals for each one. Later, you will use them as checklists to assess the apprentice's progress.

As practice, write some learning objectives with incremental goals and discuss them during a staff meeting with your business manager or shop foreman to ensure they are appropriate. The Washington State Office of the Superintendent of Public Instruction offers an excellent resource for writing workplace learning objectives: "The Worksite Learning Manual" discusses and explains how to write "SMART" worksite training objectives. The acronym stands for Specific, Measurable, Attainable, Realistic, and Time-Bound.

Specific refers to writing an understandable objective with one outcome. For instance, instead of the general "Avery will learn some parts of the 3-D software," write a more specific goal, such as, "Avery will demonstrate how to use the shaded rendering option of Rhino 3-D software."

Measurable means that the apprentice's performance can be measured. This is the function of incremental goals. Building on the previous example, we would add a task that will be used to assess the apprentice's performance. Now the objective will read, "Avery will demonstrate how to use the shaded rendering option of Rhino 3-D software by printing out 2-D images for sales staff."

Attainable refers to the apprentice's ability to attain the objective during the tenure of the apprenticeship. Write objectives that can be accomplished during a predetermined reasonable amount of time. Remember, this single objective may not be the only task in which the apprentice is to gain competency.

Realistic means that the objective is something the apprentice will be able to perform within the job setting. Do not make up objectives that are out of the context of worksite learning. Setting an objective such as "Avery will demonstrate being a trustworthy person" is unrealistic. While this trait is highly desirable in an employee, it has no direct correlation with the physical tasks the apprentice will be asked to learn in the workplace and cannot be evaluated objectively.

Time-Bound means that the apprentice adheres to a set time constraint within which to gain competency. Some objectives may take only a few hours to achieve, while others may take six weeks or more of continual practice and revision. In our revised example, the objective now contains a timeframe: "Avery will demonstrate how to use the shaded rendering option of Rhino 3-D software and print out 2-D images for sales staff by the end of July."

Well-written objectives clarify what the apprentice should be learning and ensure that the employer can assess the apprentice's progress. Use the following formula when writing an objective: "By [insert date] the apprentice will become competent in [insert task]." For instance, as part of safety training, the apprentice is required to be able to change out a gas tank for the master craftsperson's torch. Your **objective** and **goals** would read:

Objective: By the end of the first month, the apprentice will be able to safely change out gas tanks and regulators in the shop.

Goal #1. By the end of the first week, the apprentice will have read the chapter on gas and torch safety and scored 100 percent on a closed-book, written safety test.

Goal #2. By the end of the second week, the apprentice will correctly identify the parts of a compressed gas tank and regulator, and explain the safety precautions verbally to the shop foreman.

Goal #3. By the end of the third week, the apprentice will be given a hands-on demonstration of changing out a gas tank regulator and testing for leaks. The apprentice will practice the procedure with the help and guidance of an experienced goldsmith.

Goal #4. By the end of the fourth week, the apprentice will, under supervision, change out a gas tank and regulator, check for leaks, and safely store the empty cylinder.

For additional examples of breaking down training into objectives and assessable goals, see "Effective Grouping Suggestions," pages 47–52.

Effective Educational Tools

As you prepare the learning objectives and incremental goals, think about the order in which the apprentice will approach them. In the field of adult technical education, two practices—grouping and scaffolding—can help in the acquisition of knowledge.

Grouping refers to integrating related safety, procedural, and tool information with applicable skill practice and training. (All this information can be found in Chapters 4, 5, and 6.) Take the previous example of changing out a gas tank for a torch. If we were to group that learning objective with other related ones, such as learning torch control for soldering and casting applications, the apprentice's comprehension of gas and torch use would be significantly greater within a tighter timeframe.

Scaffolding means using association to further knowledge acquisition. Most people are familiar with scaffoldings used in the building trade, where temporary support structures are placed on the outside of a building during construction or repair. With educational scaffolding, you identify something the learner is already familiar with and associate (or scaffold) the new information to that familiarity. The analogy "If you know how to boil water, I can show you how to make tea" doesn't fit. Instead, think of the process this way: "If you know what boiling water looks like, then that's what to look for when vacuuming the investment for lost-wax casting." You may have never seen the investment process for lost-wax casting before, and yet now you know what to look for. New knowledge and skills are acquired and put into use more easily when the new information builds upon or is scaffolded to something with which the apprentice is already familiar. Consider how writing a SMART learning objective on drawing down wire would be made easier if the apprentice had already been trained on how to light a torch, how to pour an ingot, and how to anneal. Scaffolding previously acquired single skills to create a more complex skill set helps the apprentice make important process connections while gaining skill competency.

Effective Grouping
Suggestions

Fabrication Group

Grouping the skills of "Saw and File" with those of "Fabricate and Finish" (below) will provide a well-rounded view of any apprentice's skill level. After having the apprentice complete torch safety, tool identification, and buffer/grinder safety tests, introduce the skill sets from "Saw and File" to complete the Creating Filed Cuff Bracelets project. Then have the apprentice move on to the "Fabricate and Finish" skill set, starting with practice on solder samples in brass or copper with silver solder. Complete this group by providing shop time and materials for the apprentice to make the Slot-in-Slot Construction project. With this grouping, the apprentice should be able to work independently, asking for guidance as needed. Your objective and goals for each skill set could look as follows:

FIRST SET OF SKILLS:
Saw and File

Objective: By the end of this month, the apprentice will be able to identify and load the correct saw blade while demonstrating competency in piercing a multiple layer pattern with accuracy. The apprentice will also demonstrate filing and finishing of rough sawn edges by the correct use of hand files, needle files, sanding sticks, or flex-shaft tools.

Goal #1. By the end of the first week, the apprentice will complete the tool identification, the torch safety, and the buffer/grinder safety tests (see Chapters 4 and 5) while receiving hands-on training in sawing and filing skills. The apprentice will practice these procedures with the help and guidance of an experienced goldsmith.

Goal #2. By the end of the second week, the apprentice will demonstrate the ability to saw and file shapes from sheet stock and wire with accuracy while identifying and using the correct tools for the process.

Goal #3. By the end of the third week, the apprentice will practice sawing and filing more complex patterns (e.g., piercing a name pendant in script) while receiving hands-on training in flex-shaft and buffing machine use for finishing.

Goal #4. By the end of the fourth week, the apprentice will demonstrate sawing and filing skills by making the Creating Filed Cuff Bracelets project (page 128) until the finished project meets the workplace supervisor's standards.

SECOND SET OF SKILLS:
Fabricate and Finish

Objective: By the end of this month, the apprentice will be able to perform various sheet and wire soldering constructions with well-fitted joins while planning, filing, and finishing the Slot-in-Slot Construction project (page 160) to quality standards set by the workplace supervisor.

Goal #1. By the end of the first week, the apprentice will practice completing the soldering samples in copper or brass while receiving hands-on training in finishing edges and troubleshooting soldering problems. The apprentice will practice these procedures with the help and guidance of an experienced goldsmith.

Goal #2. By the end of the second week, the apprentice will receive hands-on training in making rivets, including information on spaced rivets. The apprentice will practice these procedures with the help and guidance of an experienced goldsmith.

Goal #3. By the end of the third week, the apprentice will demonstrate finishing edges and polishing surfaces of fabricated objects with internal saw cuts through the proper use of the flex-shaft and the buffing machine to meet shop standards.

Goal #4. By the end of the fourth week, the apprentice will demonstrate how they plan for material usage, saw complex patterns with internal saw cuts accurately, and fabricate a slot-in-slot mounting for a gemstone to shop standards.

Depending on the skill and experience level of the apprentice, the "Saw and File" and "Fabricate and Finish" objectives can be run consecutively or, for a more advanced apprentice, run concurrently. Encourage the apprentice to read the books referenced with each of the training projects to develop a broader understanding of the training they are receiving. Use the Apprentice Competency Framework (pages 57-59) to record observable work habits and skill mastery for management review.

Casting Group

To advance training in the area of casting metal, have the apprentice complete gas and torch safety tests. Since the torches for casting metal are often larger and more intimidating than standard bench torches, have the apprentice demonstrate their competence by lighting and shutting down the torches used in this process. Move on to demonstrating how to pour an ingot. Start with a strip ingot mold and establish the safety precautions required for this task. These should include the spot in the shop this task is to be done (which should have fire-retardant sheet rock or kiln brick and a ventilation hood). Demonstrate preparing the mold, pre-heating and sooting the mold, bringing the metal to a molten liquid while keeping the mold hot and keeping everything at the correct temperature during the pour. Have the apprentice practice multiple times with the strip ingot mold before introducing a reversible (upright wire/ingot) mold. Have the apprentice repeat pouring until the quality of the ingot is acceptable. Use scrap silver or bronze casting shot for training.

FIRST SET OF SKILLS:
Pouring Ingots

Objective: By the end of this month, the apprentice will be able to pour a silver ingot for milling sizing stock and drawing down wire to correct gauges.

Goal #1. By the end of the first week, the apprentice (having already passed the safety test for torch use) will be able to identify the tools and safety precautions while demonstrating the appropriate use of torches required for this task.

Goal #2. By the end of the second week, the apprentice will receive hands-on training in pouring molten metal into a strip ingot mold and a reversible upright wire/ingot mold.

Goal #3. By the end of the third week, the apprentice will practice pouring ingots in both styles of ingot molds until the ingots meet standards. The apprentice will practice the procedure with the help and guidance of an experienced goldsmith.

Goal #4. By the end of the fourth week, the apprentice will demonstrate the ability to successfully pour an ingot in both styles of molds.

SECOND SET OF SKILLS: Lost-Wax Casting

Objective: By the end of this month, the apprentice will be able to perform a lost-wax casting and clean up raw castings. (Concurrent with the ingot pouring objective.)

Goal #1. By the end of the first week, the apprentice (having already passed a safety test for the casting equipment on site) will be given a demonstration of how to sprue, invest, cast, de-invest, and clean up raw castings. The apprentice will practice these procedures with the help and guidance of an experienced goldsmith.

Goal #2. By the end of the second week, the apprentice will receive hands-on training in safety procedures for mixing investment, de-bubbling investment, initiating a burnout cycle, melting metal for casting, and de-investing.

Goal #3. By the end of the third week, the apprentice will receive hands-on training in cleaning up raw castings and finishing the cast jewelry items to specifications. The apprentice will practice the procedure with the help and guidance of an experienced goldsmith.

Goal #4. By the end of the fourth week, the apprentice will demonstrate the ability to melt metal for the successful cast of a wax model with the help and guidance of an experienced goldsmith.

THIRD SET OF SKILLS:
Milling and Draw Plate Usage

Objective: By the end of this month, the apprentice will be able to use the rolling mill to mill an ingot to specific sizes required for

repairs and to further draw down round wire. (Concurrent with the ingot-pouring objective.)

Goal #1. By the end of the first week, the apprentice (having already passed the safety test for torch use) will be given a demonstration of how to appropriately use the rolling mill and will practice milling scrap metal.

Goal #2. By the end of the second week, the apprentice will receive hands-on training in annealing scrap metal and using a draw plate.

Goal #3. By the end of the third week, the apprentice will practice identifying and addressing milling problems until the sheet stock and wire results meet standards.

Goal #4. By the end of the fourth week, the apprentice will pour sterling silver ingots and demonstrate the ability to successfully mill the ingots into sizing stock and wire.

Complete this grouping of skill sets by allowing the apprentice open shop time and materials to fabricate the Introductory Filigree Bead project (page 174).

These groupings may be ambitious for a summer high school student, but they would show the mettle of a more highly trained candidate. If there is a task for which you wish to train, use these examples as templates to make up your own objectives and goals. Remember to use the "SMART" directives for writing learning objectives (page 44) while breaking down any task for which you are considering implementing training.

Six Scaffolding *Strategies*

When training an apprentice, the strategy of scaffolding instruction is an excellent way to break up a learning experience, concept, or skill into discrete parts, and then give apprentices the assistance they need to learn each part.

1. Pre-load Vocabulary: Apprentices are given a vocabulary of tools and processes before they are expected to use or converse regarding those things.

2. Pause, Ask, Pause, Review: The master goldsmith clearly describes the purpose of a learning activity, the directions apprentices need to follow, and the learning goals they are expected to achieve.

3. Time to Talk: The master goldsmith describes or illustrates a concept, problem, or process in multiple ways to ensure understanding.

4. Show and Tell: The master goldsmith gives an apprentice a simplified version of a lesson or assignment, and then gradually increases the complexity, difficulty, or sophistication over time.

5. Visual Aids: Apprentices are given examples or models of a finished assignment, which they will then be asked to complete.

6. Tap into Prior Knowledge: The master goldsmith explicitly describes how the new skills and processes build on the knowledge and skills that apprentices either were taught in previous lessons or have learned through other life experiences (e.g., equating the look of boiling water with de-bubbling investment for casting).

Choosing a Supervisor

By far, one of the most important decisions you'll make while setting up an apprenticeship is the selection of a worksite supervisor. This is the member of your staff who will meet daily with the apprentice, offer assistance when needed, listen to the apprentice's feedback on training projects, and assess the weekly progress on learning objectives and goals. When selecting a supervisor, consider the personality type of each of your managers and goldsmiths. Simply selecting the business owner, the oldest goldsmith, or even the shop foreman may not best serve your business needs or generate the most satisfactory results. The least prudent choice would be a team member who is irritated easily by distractions, has poor communication skills, and is overburdened with a demanding workload.

The optimal candidate for a worksite supervisor would be a member of your staff who:

- Understands the full spectrum of work your company conducts
- Answers questions in a positive manner
- Fosters a strong work ethic by example
- Is approachable and non-discriminatory
- Is willing to oversee the apprentice's interactions with other employees
- Provides constructive feedback

If trying to find a single individual with all these traits sounds too daunting, perhaps one of your goldsmiths who is exceptional at problem solving and who is someone other workers in your shop turn to for advice, might be your best candidate.

Remember, the supervisor does not have to conduct the apprenticeship alone. In a small company, each employee should be brought on board with the apprenticeship project by participating in various aspects of the planning, training, or brainstorming of learning objectives. For larger firms, a team of craftspeople can work together and follow the supervisor's lead. The apprenticeship supervisor can select the staff members for this team who best exemplify the attributes listed above.

However you decide to select the worksite supervisor, it is important for that individual to interact in a welcoming way with the apprentice. The supervisor should be able to show appropriate concern for the apprentice's safety and make it clear that the apprentice's best interests are in mind.

Evaluating the Apprentice's Performance

As the program progresses, the apprentice should receive regular evaluations assessing the quality of progress toward accomplishing the established goals and objectives. Remember, the nature of an apprenticeship presupposes that the apprentice is still learning valuable skills; evaluating that individual's benefit to your business's bottom line is a bit premature.

Assessment meetings can be informal, taking place either weekly or upon completion of each objective. Begin by reviewing the learning objective. Provide support by praising improvements and efforts demonstrated. Discuss the progress the apprentice has made based on the incremental goals specified in each learning objective. Discuss the apprentice's performance in relation to work ethic and skill growth expectations. Ask for the apprentice's feedback. Did the apprentice feel the objective was too difficult, too easy? Did the apprentice gain insight into the process? When necessary, offer to help the apprentice work through a challenge, and introduce them to new ideas and techniques. It's also beneficial to involve the apprentice in the decision-making process when it's time to move on to other skill training, so the training can better relate to the apprentice's interests and career goals.

Assessments can be documented by using the incremental goals from each learning objective as checklists. The supervisor and apprentice can then both sign off on these checklists. This process will provide a clear progress report of the apprentice's new abilities. Review of these assessment documents will offer the information required to identify areas in need of additional training, so the supervisor will be better equipped to determine the apprentice's readiness to move toward new skills.

Apprentice Competency Framework

If you want to advance apprentices to the next level of training, check their performance against these charts before initiating training that may be beyond or below their skill levels. To assess an apprentice's skill level, start with the "Beginning Apprentice" column and add the abilities listed under "Intermediate Apprentice" and then "Advanced Apprentice" to find their placement for each skill set on the list.

For example, if an apprentice has good safety practices but has not passed the safety tests, you would check the "Beginning" box for that skill until the person is able to pass the tests. Likewise, if the apprentice is able to identify gemstones and has some understanding of how they might be affected during jewelry-making processes, check the "Intermediate" box for that skill.

SKILL APPLICATION	BEGINNING APPRENTICE	INTERMEDIATE APPRENTICE	ADVANCED APPRENTICE
SAFETY	Practices safety training procedures. Passed safety tests.	Identifies and applies safety precautions.	Maintains best safety practices at all times.
HAND TOOLS USE	Identifies and uses basic hand tools.	Uses power/specialty tools. Organizes bench and workstation.	Makes and/or modifies tools. Maintains tools and equipment.
JEWELER'S SAW USE	Loads a saw blade into a saw frame properly. Saws straight and curved lines with accuracy.	Saws tight angles and multiple layers with accuracy.	Saws complex patterns with internal saw cuts accurately.

SKILL APPLICATION	BEGINNING APPRENTICE	INTERMEDIATE APPRENTICE	ADVANCED APPRENTICE
FILING AND SANDING	Files and sands straight metal edges.	Files and sands curved and rectangular shapes.	Plans, files, sands, and hand polishes facets onto 3-D shapes.
TORCH USE	Identifies safety protocol, lights torches for use, and shuts down torches. Anneals metal.	Performs various sheet and wire soldering constructions with well-fitted joins.	Joins different masses and materials with different solder grades.
GEMSTONE AND METAL IDENTIFICATION	Identifies basic gemstones and metals.	Understands basic properties of gemstones and metals as they apply to jewelry-making processes.	Applies gemstone and metal understanding in cleaning jewelry and assisting the stone setter.
INGOT AND ROLLING MILL EXPERTISE	Assists with ingot molds, melting metal, and pouring ingots. Practices rolling wire and sheet.	Forges, rolls sheet, and draws metal wire down from ingots. Straightens and intentionally bends metal.	Pours an ingot from precious metals, makes sheet and/or wire to temper from ingots while conserving material.
WAX MODEL HANDLING	Identifies different types of waxes, practices injecting wax models from molds.	Modifies injected wax models, uses build-up technique with wax pen, and carves wax models.	Identifies casting issues with injection waxes and cleans up wax models in prep for casting.
CASTING	Practices to sprue wax models for casting.	Assists with spruing, investing for cast, and burnout.	Assists in casting, investment removal, and clean-up of castings.

SKILL APPLICATION	BEGINNING APPRENTICE	INTERMEDIATE APPRENTICE	ADVANCED APPRENTICE
POLISHING AND CLEANING	Identifies polishing and cleaning machines, compounds, and uses.	Uses tumble finishing, pin finishing, and buffing wheel for polishing metal in proper sequences.	Evaluates finish quality and re-polishes as needed. Uses ultrasonic and steamer for cleaning jewelry.
DESIGN	Uses basic drawing techniques and understands orthographic/architectural layout.	Has knowledge of different historical jewelry periods and design styles.	Can produce black and white renderings of jewelry to design specifications.
CAD/CAM	Has introductory experience with 3-D software and 3-D printers.	Assists with prep of digital files, prep of 3-D printer, and clean-up of printed models.	Maintains 3-D printer materials and cleans up excess resin from printed models.
WORK ACUMEN	Demonstrates ethical conduct while developing on-the-job etiquette.	Refers to a specialist as necessary. Plans work sequences.	Works cost-effectively. Estimates job costs. Controls setup problems.

Apprenticeship SUCCESS STORY

G. PHIL POIRIER
Owner, G. Phil Poirier, Taos, New Mexico

How old were you when you started making jewelry/metals?

I was 16. I had a high school teacher who had experience with soldering and forging. It was the early 1970s, and there was a lot of demand for silver and turquoise jewelry. My jewelry making became a business very fast while I was still in high school.

Did you seek other master craftsmen with whom to apprentice? In which techniques have you been trained?
I did have many opportunities with masters in their fields; through word of mouth I was able to find other master craftsmen wanting to pass on what they knew. A master engraver, master gem cutter, and a master clock maker are a few with whom I have traded skills or for whom I have done piecework while learning. I knew they had the skills I needed, and I was lucky enough to have it all work out.

Did you have help to start your business?
My father was an accountant and helped with that aspect, but most of it was on the fly. I had no retail space, so that kept my overhead down. Other local craftsmen and neighboring business owners were very helpful, but if you want to be an artist in this country, you are on your own. Until industry steps up to create training programs, there will be no funding for training.

Have you trained an apprentice?
Yes, I have had a couple of apprentices. They sought me out the same way I had sought out other craftsmen when I was first getting started. I feel a great sense of pride seeing the work of Maria Samora and Callie Shevlin [two apprentices]. I also know they would not have made it so far without their own personal drive. I'm just proud to have been a part of their path to success.

Maria Samora started with me when she was about 20, after having been told "no" several times. She started soldering chains and ended up working for me for 11 years. I trained her in everything from casting

to fabrication. She now has a thriving jewelry business in Taos, New Mexico.

Calina Shevlin was another apprentice, but never an employee. She had gotten a degree in jewelry from North Texas State [now University of North Texas] under professor Harlan Butts, a renowned enamelist, and wanted to study the rose machines for engraving. She was a very fast learner and has since gone on to become the first female specialist in guilloché. (The term refers to a series of patterns engraved in metal, from the French word for "engine turning.") Calina has also written a book on the history of guilloché, *The Definitive History of Guilloché*, a comprehensive history of the art and a compendium on engine turning.

Apprenticeship SUCCESS STORY

MARIA SAMORA
Owner, Maria Samora Studio, Taos, New Mexico

How old were you when you started making jewelry/metals?
I was 22. It was 1998; I had just moved back to Taos after college and started to take some jewelry courses through our local university, UNM [University of New Mexico]. I was very interested in making jewelry and was hoping to find someone who could teach me the art.

What kind of training did you receive or seek?
I received a scholarship for a week-long intensive course with master

goldsmith Phil Poirier. Within the first day, I was completely blown away by his knowledge and the potential of what I could learn from working with him. He taught me more in that one day than I learned in my last three semesters at college. By the third day, I built up the courage to ask if he needed any help in his shop. He didn't need anyone at the time, but after a few months I received a call to see if I was still interested.

In which techniques were you trained?

The apprenticeship and training I received was very much structured in the European manner. I started out by sweeping the floors and taking out the trash. Then I began doing very labor-intensive, repetitive work. Lots of soldering, sawing, polishing, casting, and stone setting.

Once a week, Phil encouraged me to go into his library and look through books and sketch my own pieces that he would then help me create. He was very hands-on, extremely generous with his time and willing to help me with my creations. Phil took me under his wing and taught me everything, including marketing and business strategy. It's one thing to make the art, but you also need to know how to sell it!

I started making pieces and taking them with me to my night job, which was waitressing. Customers began to comment on my work and even purchase the pieces I was wearing. This gave me the confidence to create my own line of jewelry, which shortly manifested into showing in galleries and taking my work to trade shows.

I feel so blessed to have had the opportunity to work with Phil Poirier. It has been extremely valuable in my life, and I don't think I could have obtained training like this any other way.

Have you taken on an apprentice?

My husband has been working with me for the last 10 years, and I have tried to pass down some of my knowledge in the same manner. I'd say he does a great job! Also, I currently have a new assistant with whom I'm hoping to share some of my skills.

CHAPTER 4

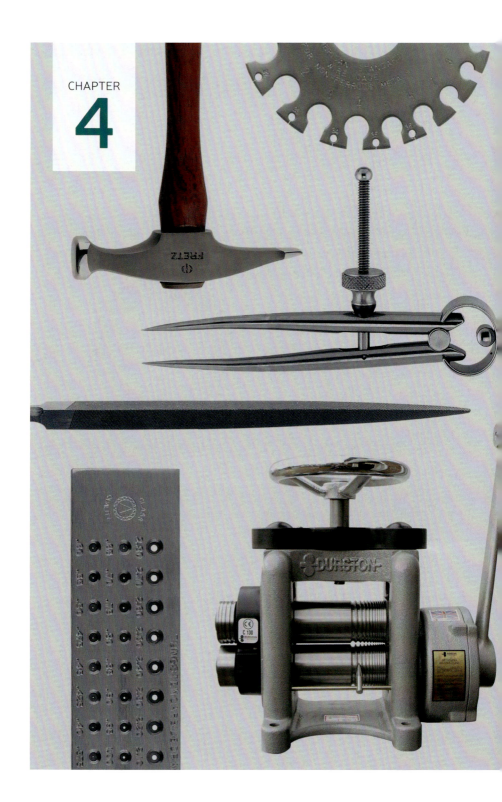

Training for
TOOL IDENTIFICATION

Testing is an important part the training process. It allows you to gauge an apprentice's knowledge and progress. It can also help the apprentice to better understand and retain key information.

This chapter provides you with a test that will help apprentices identify the common tools with which they'll be working. As any craftsman knows, it's important to have the right tools for a job—and, for an apprentice, being able to identify the right tools is crucial.

On the following pages, you'll find images of hand tools arranged into four categories: cutting tools, bending/shaping tools, measuring/marking tools, and torch tools. Above each image is a blank for the apprentice to write in the name of the tool. You can photocopy these pages to administer the test.

An answer key is provided on the last two pages of this chapter.

PHOTOCOPY THIS PAGE TO ADMINISTER THE TEST

GROUP ONE:
Cutting Tools

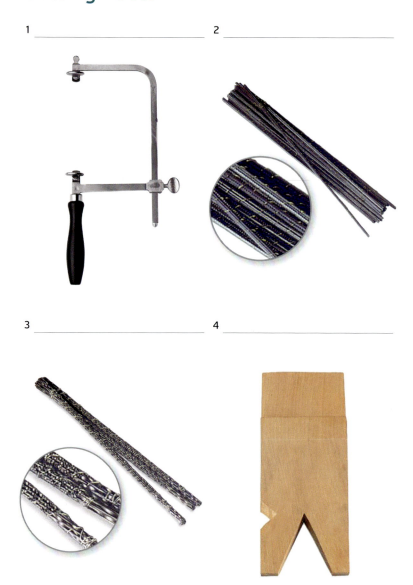

1 _____

2 _____

3 _____

4 _____

68   A JEWELER'S GUIDE TO APPRENTICESHIPS

PHOTOCOPY THIS PAGE TO ADMINISTER THE TEST

5 _____ 6 _____

7 _____ 8 _____

TRAINING FOR TOOL IDENTIFICATION

PHOTOCOPY THIS PAGE TO ADMINISTER THE TEST

9 _____ 10 _____

11 _____

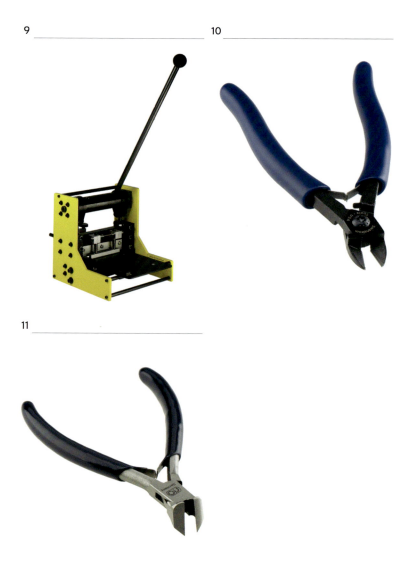

PHOTOCOPY THIS PAGE TO ADMINISTER THE TEST

GROUP TWO:
Bending/Shaping Tools

12 _____ 13 _____

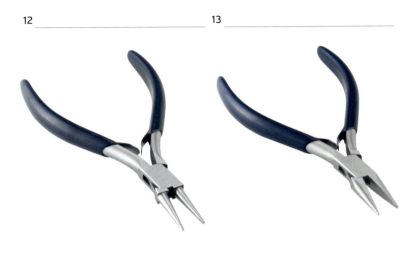

14 _____ 15 _____

TRAINING FOR TOOL IDENTIFICATION

PHOTOCOPY THIS PAGE TO ADMINISTER THE TEST

16 _____ 17 _____

18 _____ 19 _____

72 A JEWELER'S GUIDE TO APPRENTICESHIPS

PHOTOCOPY THIS PAGE TO ADMINISTER THE TEST

20 _____ 21 _____

22 _____ 23 _____

TRAINING FOR TOOL IDENTIFICATION

PHOTOCOPY THIS PAGE TO ADMINISTER THE TEST

24 _____   25 _____

26 _____   27 _____

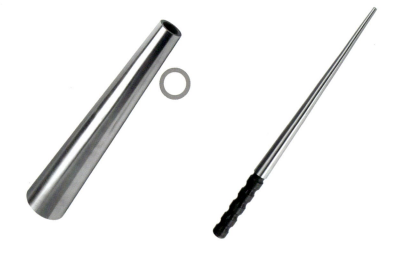

PHOTOCOPY THIS PAGE TO ADMINISTER THE TEST

28 _____   29 _____

30 _____   31 _____

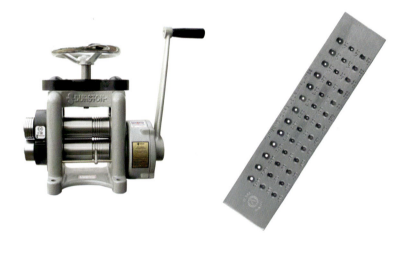
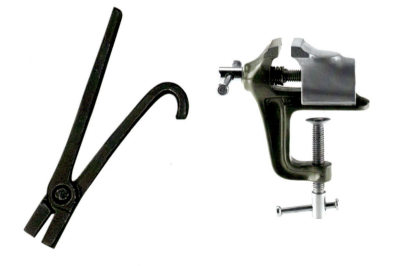

TRAINING FOR TOOL IDENTIFICATION

PHOTOCOPY THIS PAGE TO ADMINISTER THE TEST

32 _____   33 _____

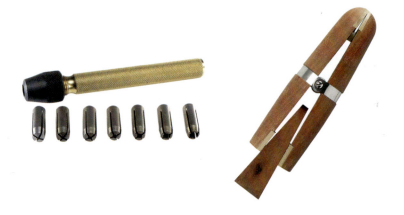

34 _____   35 _____

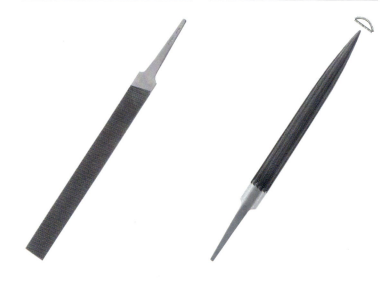

76 A JEWELER'S GUIDE TO APPRENTICESHIPS

PHOTOCOPY THIS PAGE TO ADMINISTER THE TEST

36 _____ 37 _____

38 _____ 39 _____

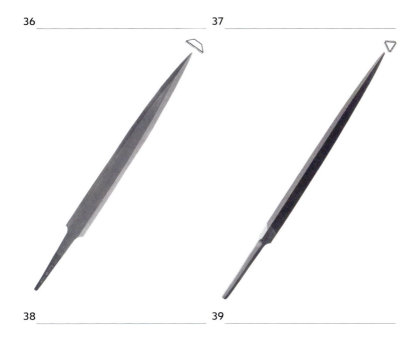

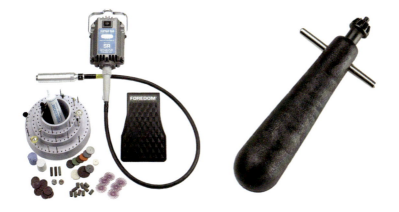

PHOTOCOPY THIS PAGE TO ADMINISTER THE TEST

40

41

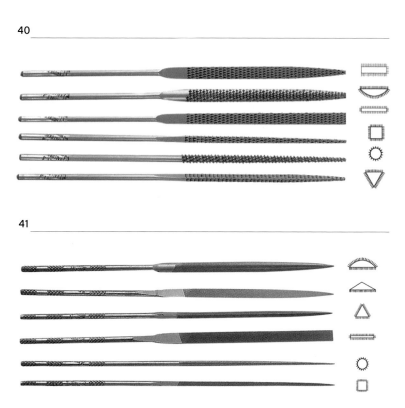

78   A JEWELER'S GUIDE TO APPRENTICESHIPS

GROUP THREE:
Measuring/Marking Tools

42 _____   43 _____

44 _____   45 _____

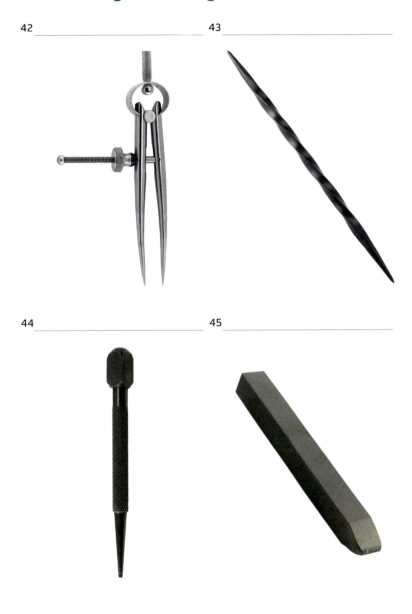

PHOTOCOPY THIS PAGE TO ADMINISTER THE TEST

46 _____ 47 _____

48 _____ 49 _____

PHOTOCOPY THIS PAGE TO ADMINISTER THE TEST

50 _____   51 _____

TRAINING FOR TOOL IDENTIFICATION

PHOTOCOPY THIS PAGE TO ADMINISTER THE TEST

GROUP FOUR:
Torch Tools

52 _____

53 _____

54 _____

55 _____

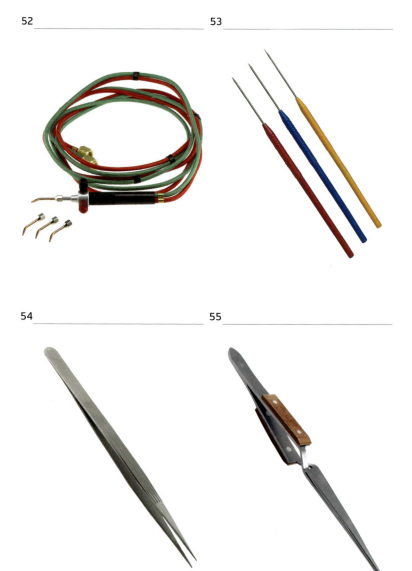

82   A JEWELER'S GUIDE TO APPRENTICESHIPS

PHOTOCOPY THIS PAGE TO ADMINISTER THE TEST

56 _____

57 _____

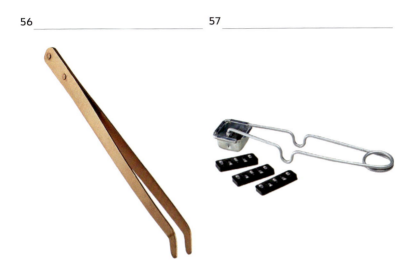

58 _____

ANSWER KEY
for Tool Identification Test

GROUP ONE:
Cutting Tools

1. Jeweler's saw frame
2. Saw blades for metal
3. Saw blades for wax
4. Bench pin
5. Miter jig (aka cutting vise)
6. Tube cutting jig
7. Disc or circle cutter
8. Hole punch
9. Guillotine shear
10. Flush cutters
11. End cutters

GROUP TWO:
Bending/Shaping Tools

12. Round-nose pliers
13. Chain-nose pliers
14. Flat-nose pliers
15. Ring bending pliers
16. Forming pliers
17. Cross-peen or riveting hammer
18. Chasing/ball-peen hammer
19. Rawhide mallet
20. Dapping punch
21. Dapping block
22. Swaging (now called "bending") block
23. Burnisher
24. Bezel roller
25. Ring mandrel
26. Bracelet mandrel
27. Bezel mandrel
28. Rolling mill
29. Draw plate
30. Draw tongs
31. Bench vise (clamp on)
32. Pin vise
33. Ring clamp
34. Flat file
35. Half-round file
36. Barrette file
37. Three-square file
38. Flex-shaft
39. Chuck key
40. Wax files
41. Needle files

GROUP THREE:
Measuring/ Marking Tools
42. Dividers
43. Scribe (double ended twist)
44. Center punch
45. Karat stamp
46. Inside ring stamp
47. Brass slide gauge
48. Degree gauge
    (aka leverage gauge)
49. Digital calipers
50. Standard sheet and wire gauge
51. Finger gauge set

GROUP FOUR:
Torch Tools
52. Torch – handpiece
53. Soldering pick
54. Utility tweezers
55. Cross-locking tweezers
56. Copper (pickle) tongs
57. Striker
58. Fuel-oxygen regulator

CHAPTER 5

Training
FOR SAFETY

Once apprentices have learned how to identify the various tools, the next step is to learn how to use them safely. In this chapter, you'll find a series of safety checkpoints that cover various shop procedures: buffing and grinding, casting, using a drill press and a hydraulic press, laser welding, and working with torches.

You'll also find tests (with answer keys) following each set of checkpoints. As in the last chapter, you can photocopy these pages to administer the tests, so apprentices can better understand how to model safe behaviors.

On the next page, you'll find an agreement identifying general safety rules that should be followed in the shop at all times. Photocopy this page and ask the apprentices to sign at the bottom, to show they understand the importance of behaving safely in the shop at all times.

PHOTOCOPY THIS PAGE TO ADMINISTER THE TEST

Safety Rules for Jewelry Manufacturing

The following agreement should be photocopied for the apprentices to sign before they begin to pick up tools. It states unequivocally the importance of safe behaviors in the shop.

1. *SAFETY GLASSES MUST BE WORN* WHEN WORKING WITH TOOLS, EQUIPMENT, TORCHES, AND CHEMICALS!

2. *NO OPEN-TOED SHOES!* NO SANDALS! NO FLIP FLOPS! Closed-toed shoes are the only type of footwear permitted in the jewelry room.

3. *LONG HAIR MUST BE TIED BACK* IN A BRAID OR PONYTAIL AT ALL TIMES!

4. Breaking or damaging any equipment, tools, or samples will result in disciplinary action!

5. Do not polish chains, wire, or cables on the polishing machine!

6. Do not use any tool or piece of equipment unless you have received permission and have passed the safety test for that tool.

7. Do not use any tool for anything other than its proper and designated purpose. Treat every tool with respect.

Failure to abide by these rules will result in your removal from this position.

Signature: _____

PHOTOCOPY THIS PAGE TO ADMINISTER THE TEST

General Safety Test

1. You should *only* use a piece of equipment if you have received _____ and you have _____ _____ _____ _____.

2. Loose clothing should be _____ before working with tools and machines. Long sleeves should be _____ _____.

3. _____ toed shoes are the only form of footwear permitted in the jewelry room. _____ are not allowed.

4. When working with *any* tool in the jewelry room, you should always wear _____ _____.

5. All loose, dangling chains, bracelets, or earrings should be _____ before working on a tool.

6. Long hair should be _____ _____ during work at all times.

7. Failure to treat the tools with _____ may result in personal injury and dismissal from employment.

See page 118 for answer key.

Casting Equipment

Safety Checkpoints

• Jewelers typically use either centrifugal or vacuum casting machines. A centrifugal casting machine uses the weight of the metal and centrifugal force to fill the mold. A vacuum casting machine uses a vacuum to suck the molten metal into the mold.

• A centrifugal machine must be securely bolted to a level surface, with a protective splatter shield installed around it. To avoid injury, do not reach into the protective splatter shield while the centrifugal casting machine is in motion.

• To prevent molten metal from blowing out or spilling, balance the casting arm of a centrifugal casting machine to each flask before casting. Unless all the flasks are equal, the weights must be changed to balance each flask. Follow these basic steps:

1. Place the invested (but not burnt-out) flask into the centrifugal machine.
2. Slide the crucible to the mold and put your pre-measured metal for that flask into the crucible.
3. Loosen the center nut so the arm will teeter-totter.
4. Adjust the counter-balance weights so a slight touch will cause the arm to move up or down equally on each side.
5. Make sure that you tighten the weight nut and the center nut. Check them again and then once more just to be sure.

• Either a vacuum or a centrifugal machine should be at a comfortable working height. Remember, you'll be working with hot flasks, molten metal, and a

Centrifugal Casting Machine

blazing torch. You will not want to contort yourself into uncomfortable or unsafe positions. Make sure the burnout kiln, casting machine, and torches are placed in the safest and most ergonomic arrangement.

• Always wear eye protection. When casting, the torch flames and molten metal will be hotter than when soldering; a tinted lens is advisable. Use tinted safety glasses in a 2 to 4 range, which will block ultra-violet (UV) light, infrared (IR) radiation, and sodium flare.

• For either casting machine, flasks must be prepared and filled with investment plaster. Casting investments contain high levels of cristobalite, a high-temperature polymorph of silica, which—if inhaled—can cause silicosis, a lung disease. It is necessary to have ventilation and wear a dust-filtering mask when handling investment and wet mopping all surface areas to remove the residual dust.

Buffing and Grinding Machines

Safety Checkpoints: Buffing Machines

• *NO CHAINS, NO WIRE, NO CABLES* are allowed on the buffing machine! These items will catch in the buff and can amputate fingers.

• *EYE PROTECTION* should always be worn when using this machine.

• *LONG HAIR* should always be tied back. It can get caught in the buff and cause serious injury.

• Make sure all loose clothing and jewelry is tied back, securely tucked in, or removed before working on the buffing machine. This includes hoody strings, scarfs, chains, long sleeves, and bracelets.

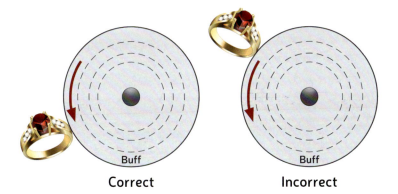

Correct   Incorrect

• Buff using only the lower front quarter on the downward rotation of the buffing wheel. Other areas of the buff will catch the metal and throw it, causing injuries and damaging the jewelry piece.

• Do not work on this machine without proper ventilation.

• If there is anything wrong with the machine, turn it off, unplug it, and alert your supervisor.

• The buffing machine is used to polish *METAL*. Other materials will contaminate and ruin the buffs. Rouge polishing buffs will not remove scratches from the metal—they will only make the scratches shine.

• Buffing compound is a very fine abrasive compound. It will cause the metal to *HEAT* up. This means that, if you press too hard against the buff, you will *BURN* yourself.

• Do not put *ABRASIVE COMPOUND* on a *POLISHING BUFF*. Abrasive compounds will contaminate the polishing buffs and scratch your piece.

• Always clean off your metal with detergent and water before moving from one buff to another.

• Use this machine only after training and passing the safety test.

Safety Checkpoints: Grinding Machines

• Grinding machines are used to alter or sharpen steel tools. Wear safety glasses or a face shield whenever using a grinding machine.

• Before using the machine, secure long hair; tuck in or remove loose clothing, including long sleeves, scarfs, and hoodie strings; and remove long chains and bracelets.

Buffing Machine

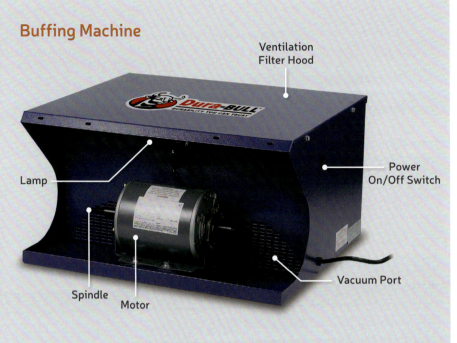

Grinding Machine

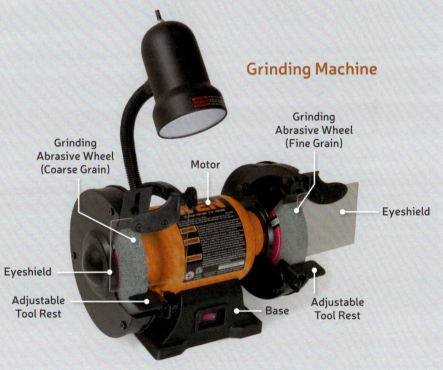

- Use proper wheel guards on all grinding machines.

- On bench grinders, adjust the tool rest to within $1/16$ to $1/8$ inch from the wheel.

- The tool rest should be stationed in the lower quarter of the downward rotation on the grinding wheel.

- Never adjust the wheel guard or tool rest when the machine is running.

- Check the grinding wheel for cracks before mounting it on the spindle and before starting the machine.

- Never operate grinding wheels at speeds that exceed the manufacturer's recommendation.

- Do not exceed the recommended depth of cut.

- Remove the workpiece from the grinding wheel before turning off the machine.

- After turning off the machine, allow the grinding wheel to come to a natural stop. Do not try to stop it or slow it down.

PHOTOCOPY THIS PAGE TO ADMINISTER THE TEST

Buffing Machine/Grinding Wheel Safety Test

1. Name three items that are not allowed on a buffing machine.
   A. _____
   B. _____
   C. _____

2. Buffing _____ is a very fine _____. It will cause the metal to _____ up. This means if you press too hard against the buff you will _____ yourself.

3. Use either _____ or _____ machines only after passing the _____ _____ .

4. Make sure all _____ clothing and jewelry is tied back, securely tucked in, or removed before working on the buffing machine or grinding wheel.

5. Name three things that should be secured or removed before working on either tool:
   A. _____
   B. _____
   C. _____

6. Always wear _____ _____ when working with these tools.

TRAINING FOR SAFETY

PHOTOCOPY THIS PAGE TO ADMINISTER THE TEST

7. The buffing machine is used to _____ metal.

8. The grinding machine is used to _____ or _____ metal tools.

9. If there is anything wrong with the machine, _____ _____ _____, unplug it, and call your _____.

10. If you are not careful, the buffing/grinding wheel will:
  A. Catch the metal and throw it.
  B. Cause possible severe injury.
  C. Damage tools and jewelry.
  D. All of the above.

11. The only area of the buffing/grinding wheel you should use is:
  A. The top rear quarter on the upward rotation.
  B. The lower front quarter on the downward rotation.
  C. The lower rear quarter on the upward rotation.
  D. The top front quarter on the downward rotation.

See page 118 for answer key.

Drill Presses

Safety Checkpoints

• Always wear eye protection, either safety glasses (with side shields) or a face shield.

• Remove loose-fitting clothing and jewelry. Do not wear gloves or anything that might get wrapped around the revolving bit and cause injury to hands or fingers.

• Tie back long hair.

• Center-punch the drill-hole location into the stock.

• Make all drill press adjustments with the power shut off.

• Keep all guards and covers on the machine when it is running.

• Make sure that the size of the bit is equal to or less than the capacity of the drill press, and that the bit is rated for the material you are drilling. Do not use wood drill bits on metal.

• Insert the bit into the drill chuck and tighten with the chuck key in at least two of the three sockets. Remove the chuck key from the drill chuck before starting the drill press.

• Support the underside of the stock to be drilled with a backing board secured to the drill press table. For large pieces of metal, use a clamp to securely fasten the stock and board. To secure round or irregularly shaped stock, use a "V" block clamp.

• Clear the drill table of everything except the stock you are drilling and the backing board.

• When drilling deep holes, frequently raise the drill bit from the hole to cool the bit and, with a bench brush, remove cuttings.

• If a drill bit binds, do not grab it. Turn off the drill press and carefully turn the drill chuck backwards by hand to free the bit.

• Never use your hands or fingers to stop the rotation of the drill chuck, spindle, or stock. Never reach around or under a rotating drill bit, or grab the chuck to stop a drill press. This can result in hand puncture or other serious injuries.

• Turn off the drill press before looking up or walking away from the machine.

• After turning off the machine, don't touch the drill bit and shavings, since they may be hot immediately after drilling.

• Clean the drill press table and the work area upon completion of drilling. Always use a bench brush; do not use your hands or blow the drill shavings.

Drill Press

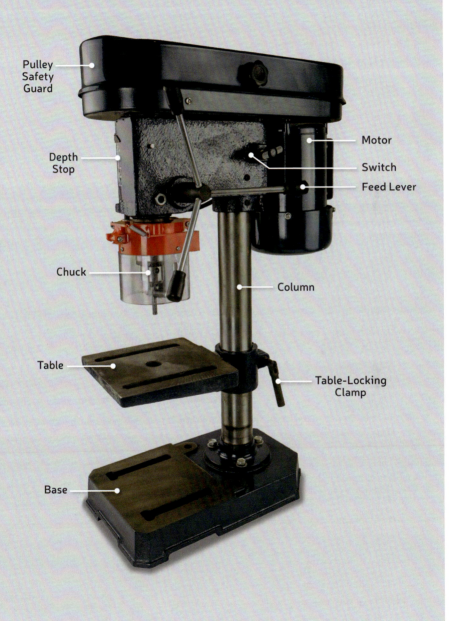

PHOTOCOPY THIS PAGE TO ADMINISTER THE TEST

Drill Press Safety Test

1. Objects other than the backing board support and your metal should be _____ from the drill table.

2. The type of drill bit you select for drilling should be rated for _____.

3. Use a _____ to secure round or irregularly shaped stock.

4. Always use a _____ _____ to locate the desired location of the drill hole.

5. If a drill bit binds on your metal, do not _____ it. Turn the machine _____. Allow the drill to come to a complete _____ before turning the drill chuck _____ by hand to remove your metal.

6. Always remove metal chips from the drill press table with a _____ _____ and never your _____.

7. Before operating the drill press or any power tool in the jewelry shop, you should take the following safety precautions (list three):

    A. _____
    B. _____
    C. _____

PHOTOCOPY THIS PAGE TO ADMINISTER THE TEST

8. When drilling, always use a _____ _____ under your metal to _____ it.

9. As with any tool, if it is not working properly you should _____ _____ _____ and inform your _____.

10. Proper _____ _____ must be worn at all times when operating a drill press.

11. Never try to stop the _____ with your hands or fingers.

12. Always remove the _____ _____ from the drill chuck before starting the drill press.

See page 118 for answer key.

Hydraulic Presses

Safety Checkpoints

• The press frame should be bolted down to a sturdy worktable or bench.

• Stand to the frame side of the press and wear safety glasses. To avoid injury, do not stand in front of the open face of the press. Should a tool break or become dislodged, standing in front of the open face will expose you to flying shrapnel.

• Never exceed the maximum rating for the jack while pumping, and never pull on the pump handle until it bends. A 20-ton jack is rated at slightly less than 9,000 psi (pounds/square inch). For safe operation, always check the pressure gauge, watch what is happening inside the platens, and listen for strange noises.

• The frame must be square so that the platens are perfectly parallel to each other. The platens must be flat with no uneven surfaces.

• Place all work at dead center in the press. This will keep the platens from tilting, which would allow tools and metal to shoot out of the press. To make sure your work is centered, look at each side from a 90 degree angle.

• Release pressure if the platens tilt in any way.

• Never use tools in the press that were not intended for it. Cast-iron raising stakes may shatter under pressure.

Hydraulic Press

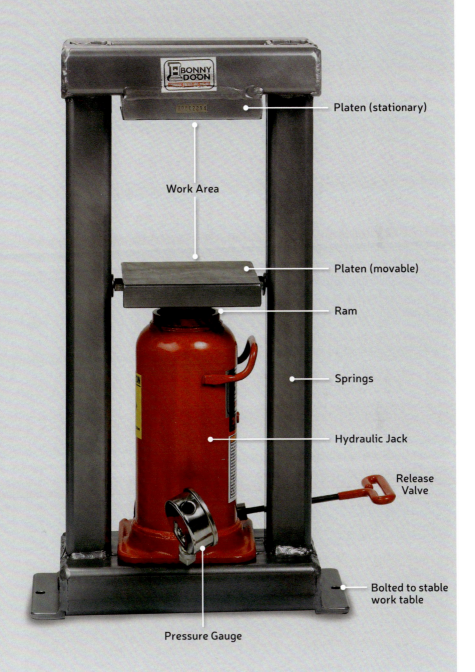

• Never operate a hydraulic press (or any machine) if you are in a fatigued state or under the influence of alcohol or drugs, including prescription medications.

Maintenance Procedures

• Do not overextend the ram of the jack during use.

• There should be at least six inches of workspace between the platens.

• Use acrylic spacers to fill the space between the platens so you do not overextend the ram.

• Do not use hard (white) urethane as a spacer. Although it may feel as hard as acrylic, it will flex under pressure, breaking acrylic silhouette dies and bending steel ones.

• When done working with the press, always lower the jack completely and close the release valve. The ram has hydraulic oil on it and will collect dust and grit, which will damage the jack.

PHOTOCOPY THIS PAGE TO ADMINISTER THE TEST

Hydraulic Press Safety Test

1. Never use tools in the press that _____ _____ _____ _____ _____ .

2. Do not overextend the _____ of the jack during use of the hydraulic press.

3. When placing work in the hydraulic press, it should be _____ _____ .

4. To make sure you never exceed the maximum rating for the hydraulic press, you need to check the _____ .

5. Before operating the hydraulic press, the frame must be _____ _____ and the _____ must be level and flat with no _____ surfaces.

6. To check if your work is _____ in the hydraulic press you should look at it from _____ to _____ .

See page 119 for answer key.

Laser Equipment

Safety Checkpoints

• Radiation produced by laser light is capable of vaporizing, burning, or melting most materials, as well as flesh. Additionally, depending on the composition of the metal alloys in the jewelry you're welding, the laser can generate hazardous vapors and gases. *Follow all safety instructions and information outlined in the laser's operating manual.*

• Always use laser eyewear that will provide protection from direct, reflective, and scattered radiation.

• Carry out all necessary inspections and maintenance work recommended by the laser manufacturer.

• Trainees must be supervised by an experienced laser operator.

• Read and understand the current OSHA regulations on "Safe Use of Lasers" regarding accident prevention and laser radiation.

• Check all safety mechanisms on the laser to make sure they are functioning properly and mounted correctly. Only use the laser welder if all such mechanisms are in proper working order.

• Do not use the laser if you see damage to the welding chamber/area door, enclosures, protective flaps, guards, welding chamber/view window, or any structure that could allow laser energy to exit the device.

• Do not use a designated jewelry-metals laser on non-metallic materials, especially plastics.

• Do not make any modifications or additions to the laser housing.

• To avoid noxious welding vapors, use the correct inert gas as directed in the operating manual.

• Never trigger a laser pulse while your fingers or hands are directly under the crosshairs of the stereo microscope in the welding chamber.

• Do not use this tool for anything other than its specific purpose.

Safe Torch Procedures

Basic Torch Styles

• **Air-fuel torch (also known as atmospheric/fuel torch or blowtorch).** This torch, for use with a single tank, is easily identifiable because it has a single regulator, a single pressure gauge, and a single fuel hose. The pressure of the gas fuel moving through the torch handpiece pulls air from the atmosphere, and it can be ignited upon exiting the torch tip.

• **Oxy-fuel torch.** This torch is identified by two sets of gas tanks, regulators, and gas hoses. One set is for compressed oxygen, and the other is for the compressed fuel. This style of torch allows for greater adjustability of the flame. Once you have established which hoses go with which fuel, *do not switch them*: The hoses may still contain by-product residue from the previous gas, and mixing with another fuel could lead to an explosion.

Gases Commonly Used with Jeweler's Torches

• **Compressed Natural Gas (CNG)** is stored in high-pressure tanks (3,000 to 3,600 psi). Natural gas consists mostly of **methane** and is drawn from gas wells or produced in conjunction with crude-oil processing. As delivered through a pipeline system, it can also contain hydrocarbons, such as ethane and propane, as well as other gases, such as nitrogen, helium, carbon dioxide, sulfur compounds, and water vapor. A sulfur-based odorant is normally added to CNG to facilitate leak detection. Natural gas is lighter than air, and thus will normally dissipate in the case of a leak, giving it a significant safety advantage over propane.

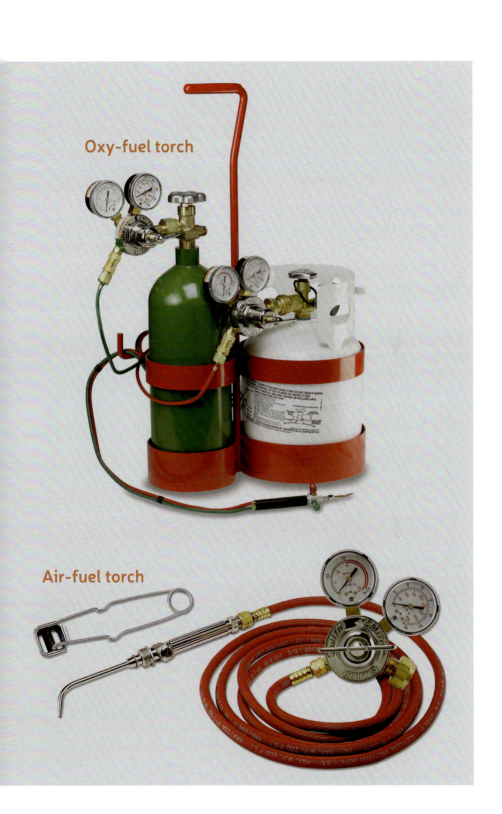

Oxy-fuel torch

Air-fuel torch

- **Liquefied Petroleum Gas (LPG)** consists mainly of **propane**, propylene, butane, and butylene in various mixtures. It is produced as a by-product of natural gas processing and petroleum refining. The components of LPG are gases at normal temperatures and pressures. One challenge with LPG is the fact that, unlike natural gas, LPG is heavier than air, and thus will flow along floors and tend to settle in low spots, such as basements. Such accumulations can cause explosion hazards.

- **Hydrogen** (H_2 gas) is highly flammable and will burn at concentrations as low as 4 percent H_2 in air. In a water torch (suitable for gold applications), hydrogen is produced from the electrolysis of water—water is electronically broken down into hydrogen and oxygen gas molecules, then piped to a torch handpiece for ignition. Otherwise, hydrogen is stored in high-pressure tanks and used primarily with compressed oxygen when casting platinum and palladium. The compressed gas tanks should be chained to a wall or a stable object to ensure they don't fall, which could lead to rupture and an explosive hazard. Keep the tanks free of grease and dirt.

- **Acetylene** (C_2H_2 gas) is non-explosive when dissolved in acetone; it is stored in this state under pressure in steel cylinders. Always use and store the acetylene cylinder in an upright position or the gas could disassociate, which could lead to an explosive chemical reaction. Tanks should be chained to a wall or a stable object, and kept free of grease and dirt.

The gas also tends to disassociate when used above 15 psi, which, again, could lead to an explosive reaction.

When mixed with compressed oxygen (oxy/acetylene), the resulting flame brightness becomes a danger to unprotected vision. This gas is too hot to make it a fuel of choice for daily professional jewelry applications. (Oxy/acetylene mixtures can reach up to 3,500 degrees Celsius or in excess of 6,300 degrees Fahrenheit, and is primarily used for cutting and welding steel.) Yet, due to its lower cost, it's a popular fuel with jewelry programs and craft centers using an atmospheric/fuel style torch. An apprentice may have experience only with this style of gas torch.

FUEL GAS	W/COMPRESSED OXYGEN	W/ ATMOSPHERIC AIR
ACETYLENE	3,500°C – 6,330°F	2,500°C – 4,500°F
HYDROGEN	3,200°C – 5,800°F	2,210°C – 4,010°F
NATURAL GAS (METHANE)	2,500°C – 4,500°F	1,600°C – 2,900°F
PROPANE	2,530°C – 4,600°F	1,990°C 3,600°F

Before Going to the Soldering Bench...

• Make sure all joints meet cleanly without gaps. No light should be visible through the seams.

• Prepare all metal to be soldered: File and sand connecting parts, pickle any discolored metal, and scrub with a brass brush and soap.

Before Turning on the Gas...

• Clear away all paper and other flammables from your workspace, tie back long hair, roll back baggy sleeves, and put on proper eye protection.

• Practice getting a spark from the striker.

• Paint flux on all parts that will be joined.

• Select the correct solder—hard, medium, or easy.

• Place solder so that it touches both pieces of metal.

• Place the torch in your non-dominant hand, and have the striker ready near your dominant hand.

Once the Gas Is On...

• Quickly take up the striker and light the gas. Adjust the torch flame's intensity with oxygen.

• Focus the inside, light blue, cone tip on the metal to be joined. Be careful not to get too close, as "puddling" the flame is less effective and may cause the torch to backfire.

• When working on silver, copper, and brass, heat up the whole metal assembly. With gold, palladium, and platinum, focus a more intense flame on the joint.

• Solder will flow to where direct heat is greatest.

• Watch for the solder to show along the joint. Look for a shiny liquid at the seam.

• When finished, first turn off the oxygen, then the gas.

After Turning Off the Gas...

• Use tweezers or tongs to pick up metal.

• Quench the hot metal in the water-filled quench pot.

• Transfer the cooled metal from the quench pot to the pickle pot by hand.

PHOTOCOPY THIS PAGE TO ADMINISTER THE TEST

Torch Work Safety Test

1. Identify two types of torches by name and distinct characteristics.

    A. _____

    B. _____

2. Before soldering, you need to make sure that the metal is _____ and the seams meet without any_____.

3. Name three safety procedures you should follow before turning on the gas of the torch handpiece.

    A. _____

    B. _____

    C. _____

4. Keep all _____ materials AWAY from the soldering area.

5. Keep all compressed gas tanks free of _____ and _____.

6. Use _____ to pick up the HOT metal.

7. To cool the hot metal off, place it in the _____ filled quench pot at the bench. Transfer the cooled metal to the _____ pot by hand.

8. Hold the torch in your _____ - _____ hand and use the striker with your _____ hand.

9. Proper _____ protection must be _____ when soldering.

PHOTOCOPY THIS PAGE TO ADMINISTER THE TEST

10. LPG consists mainly of _____ and is heavier than _____.

11. When soldering, the solder MUST touch _____ pieces of metal.

12. The compressed gas tanks are fastened with chain to a wall or stable object to protect against _____ _____.

13. Never _____ hoses from one fuel to another as the gas by-product residue may cause an _____ hazard.

14. When shutting off a torch, always turn off _____ first.

See page 119 for answer key.

Test Answer Keys

General Safety Test

1. Permission, passed the safety test
2. Secured or removed, rolled back
3. Closed, sandals or flip flops
4. Safety glasses
5. Removed
6. Tied back
7. Respect

Buffing Machine/Grinding Wheel Safety Test

1. No chains, no wires, no cables
2. Compound, abrasive, heat, burn
3. Buffing, grinding, safety test
4. Loose
5. Any of the following: long hair, loose clothing (long sleeves, scarfs, hoodie strings), bracelets, long chains
6. Eye protection
7. Polish

8. Alter, sharpen
9. Turn it off, supervisor
10. D, all of the above
11. B, the lower front quarter on the downward rotation

Drill Press Safety Test

1. Cleared or removed
2. Metal
3. V-clamp
4. Center punch
5. Grab, off, stop, backwards
6. Bench brush, hands
7. Wear safety glasses, remove or secure loose clothing, tie back long hair
8. Backing board, support
9. Turn it off, supervisor
10. Eye protection
11. Drill or chuck
12. Chuck key

Test Answer Keys

Hydraulic Press Test
1. Were not intended for it
2. Ram
3. Dead center
4. Pressure gauge
5. Bolted down, platens, uneven
6. Centered, side to side

Torch Work Safety Test
1. Air-fuel torch (or atmospheric/fuel torch, blowtorch) with single regulator, tank, and hose. Oxy-fuel torch with two tanks, two regulators, and two hoses
2. Clean, gaps
3. Clear away all flammables, tie back long hair, roll back baggy sleeves, have the striker ready, wear proper eye protection
4. Flammable
5. Grease and dirt
6. Tongs, tweezers
7. Water, pickle
8. Non-dominant, dominant
9. Eye, worn
10. Propane, air
11. Both
12. Falling over or explosive hazard
13. Switch, explosive
14. Oxygen

Apprenticeship SUCCESS STORY

AMBER WORLEY
Jewelry Designer/Metalsmith, Green Lake Jewelry Works, Seattle

How old were you when you started making jewelry/metals?
Around the age of 23 years old, at the Art Institute of Seattle.

Please talk about your entry into the jewelry business.
I took one basic metals class at the Art Institute with Nanz Aalund. Before I graduated, I had an informational interview with Nanz, during which she let me know that I was choosing a difficult path. I didn't doubt her experience in the jewelry industry, but I knew that this was what I wanted to do.

I moved home to Boise, Idaho, and interviewed at every jewelry store in town, but no one would hire a female jeweler. Their reasons included "women don't want to get their hands dirty" and the belief that women will give up their profession when they get married and have babies. I became so frustrated with my search that I almost joined the Marines.

I moved back to Seattle and, after a year of searching, found Green Lake Jewelry Works [a specialist in custom jewelry]. I stopped in every day to speak with the owner, Jim Tuttle. After two weeks, he finally invited me for an interview. He hired me as a designer for the sales floor. I started working on rough sketches and the conceptual stages of custom jewelry, and within a year I was given a jeweler's bench. It was less of an apprenticeship and more of "figure it out, or you can't have a bench."

What kind of goldsmithing training did you receive or seek at Green Lake?

My mentors over the years have been Robbie Curnow, Henry Nguyen, and Joe Worley, who would become my husband. Each one is a master jeweler with the highest level of integrity. They taught me the soldering process of gold and platinum, the subtleties of polishing, basic fabrication, and filigree. They have never compromised the quality of their work and are honest, hardworking jewelers.

Over the next 10 years at Green Lake, I learned every setting style and became the lead filigree artist. I even taught myself basic engraving. In the future, I plan to explore engraving further and figure out my artistic voice through this method.

If you decided to open your own business, how would you acquire the necessary skills?

I have dabbled with two business concepts, but found that, at this time in my life, I am not ready to jump into owning a business. I find comfort in having an established workplace to go to and in being able to leave at the end of the day. However, I would want to take some business classes to gain confidence in these areas.

Was there a jewelers' union you had to join when you started? Would having one have helped?

No, there was not a jewelers' union at the time I entered the industry. I would have loved it if there had been one. I feel like we are losing the craft because so few business owners are willing to pay master jewelers what they are worth. It seems that "big box" jewelry stores are mainly looking just for "good enough" for the lowest pay possible. It is my thinking that if there were a union, there would be more accountability, and it might revive the craft for younger jewelers. For those just starting out, it could provide a path, so they'd know that there will be an upward momentum throughout their careers.

Did your mentors establish specific goals or objectives for your training?

I wasn't given a choice, and it was more of an on-the-job training without a real plan. I was paid an hourly rate at minimum wage without commission or bonus for the first five years. We were building this  side of the business as the store gained momentum. My training was completely up to me and how hard I wanted to push myself. Every year, I determined a new skill set to learn and worked on it until it became second nature.

Have you taken on an apprentice?

Yes, I have taken on two female apprentices. It was very trying, but rewarding as well. It helped me to realize just how far I had come with my own skills. It tested my knowledge, and I enjoyed sharing everything with my coworkers because I knew how hard it is to get a bench, especially for a woman.

CHAPTER 6

In this chapter, you'll find illustrated projects that will show the apprentice, in detail, how to perform specific tasks that will enable them to gain proficiency.

- Basic Soldering: Practice Exercises (page 125)
- Creating Filed Cuff Bracelets (page 128)
- Wax Carving (page 138)
- Rivet Capture Pendant (page 148)
- Slot-in-Slot Construction (page 160)
- Introductory Filigree Bead (page 174)

Basic Soldering: Practice Exercises

Gaining skill in torch control and accurate solder flow are basic "must have" skills for anyone wanting to pursue advanced jewelry making and achieve reliable craftsmanship. These exercises have been developed to teach apprentices what to look at and what to look for while learning to lead a complete solder flow with the torch tip, regardless of fuels or torch setups.

How to Use This Project

Have the apprentice practice completing these seven soldering samples in copper and brass with silver solders of hard, medium, and easy. Inspect the metal and seams for solder puddles, pits, and gaps. Use obvious soldering problems to direct additional instruction. Have the apprentice fabricate projects in copper or brass before advancing to silver. Build on skill level advancement by refining the scale and complexity of soldering procedures. Allow the apprentice to advance to the Slot-in-Slot Construction or the Introductory Filigree Bead projects as their skill level indicates.

Using These Exercises to Assess Skill Level

These solder exercises can be used during an interview process as a bench test for more advanced apprentice candidates. Provide the candidate with materials and a fully supplied bench to complete these seven exercises as quickly and cleanly as possible for their skill level. Compare the apprentice candidate's performance with the Apprentice Competency Framework (pages 57-59). Questions to ask during assessment:

- Were safety procedures followed?
- Are the solder joins clean?
- Did the apprentice waste time or material?
- How long did the apprentice take to complete all seven soldering exercises?

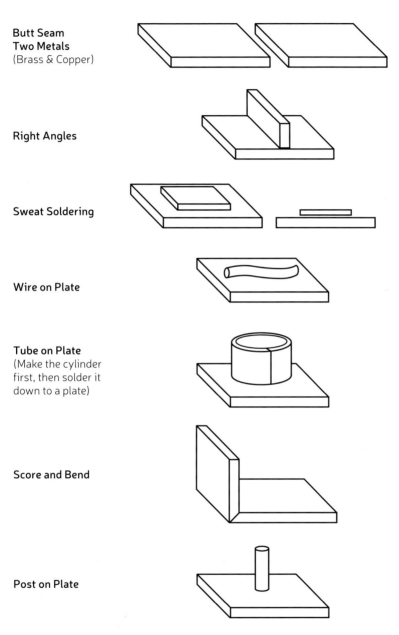

Butt Seam Two Metals (Brass & Copper)

Right Angles

Sweat Soldering

Wire on Plate

Tube on Plate (Make the cylinder first, then solder it down to a plate)

Score and Bend

Post on Plate

For additional information, see *The Complete Metalsmith* by Tim McCreight and *The Theory and Practice of Goldsmithing* by Dr. Erhard Brepohl.

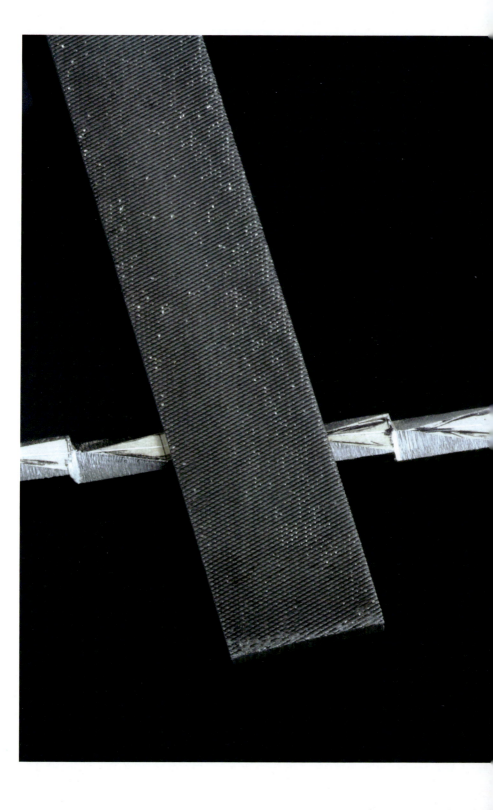

Creating FILED CUFF BRACELETS

Hand files and all the various styles of files are basic tools for shaping sheet and wire stock in all the jewelry metals. The proper, controlled use of files for a repeatable, desired result is a mark of quality craftsmanship. This chapter features a project that offers an excellent way to practice and develop this skill. Presented by Sam Patania of Patania's Sterling Silver Originals in Tucson, Arizona, it focuses on the development of two cuff bracelets with filed patterns. An added creative challenge in applying this technique would be to experiment with how many different variations of patterns are possible.

How to Use This Project

When using this project for skill training, group it with rolling mill training. Patania recommends that for this cuff, the 6-gauge square wire needs to be as straight and flat as possible. For a beginning apprentice, being able to mill out the square wire stock to the project specifications could be set as an objective to accomplish before progressing to the filing of patterns. Or while the apprentices work toward successfully milling the square silver wire for this project, they can also practice filing patterns on square copper rod stock. After the apprentices have completed a practice bracelet in copper, have them progress to the silver they have milled for the project.

Since speed, accuracy, and innovation improve with practice, look for speed of completion and more developed file patterns when using this project to assess intermediate skill levels.

Skills:
- Marking and measuring to plan
- Use of dividers
- Accurate filing technique

Materials:
- 6 inches of 6-gauge square wire

Tools:
- Dividers
- Files:
  Rough-cut, square (00 – 1 cuts)
  Triangle (2 cut)
  Bastard-cut, flat (00 – 1 cut)
  Double half-round (2 cut)
- 3-inch saw frame with 2/0 blade
- Bench pin secured to a heavy, steady bench with a bench light
- Checkering File

Hand Filing Techniques
By Sam Patania

The basic idea behind hand filing is to smooth and shape metal, and even to possibly add textures and create interesting patterns. Always, you'll want to go down just to the cut line (i.e., the outside edge of your design) and no farther. Which is why, if you trace a design template on the metal and cut it out with a hand saw, you always want to cut just outside the line's edge. This is called "leaving your line" and it will provide the cushion you need to achieve the desired finishes and textures.

For the cuff in this project, the 6-gauge square wire needs to be as straight and flat as possible. As you file, remember that a bench pin has two surfaces: the filing surface, which slopes down, and the sawing surface, which is flat and parallel to the bench. I teach students to switch between them as needed, and to avoid filing on the sawing surface—if they don't switch, the bench pin's edges will soon become slanted and begin interfering with saw strokes.

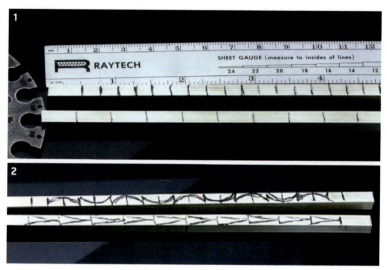

IMAGE 1: *After using dividers to find the center of the wire stock, mark off 0.25 to 0.5 inch increments.* IMAGE 2: *The designs (one triangular, one scalloped) traced onto the silver wire stock.*

Creating Filed Cuff Bracelets

This type of design is created by removing metal from the original stock. To find the center, I always use my dividers, not a ruler. The dividers give a much better picture of the center of a piece of silver than the ruler. Then I radiate out from the center in 0.25 to 0.5 inch increments to the ends (see Image 1). I have tried to use a more detailed layout, but find that this is the most useful method. I mark the lines on the top and sides of the square wire. I also lay out the center along the length of the wire stock on all three sides that I am going to be filing—the top and two sides—skipping what will become the inside of the cuff (see Image 2).

To leave a line down the middle, I find the center of any piece of sterling stock by using my dividers and marking from opposite sides of the stock.

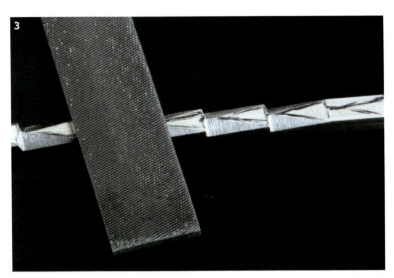

IMAGE 3: *Use a bastard-cut file to file the triangular design into the silver, with the cutting edge digging into the metal.*

I often must adjust the dividers so they make a single line through the center of the stock. I open the dividers and make test marks on the underside of my silver until I can mark the center of the working side. Since the refining industry in the U.S. uses English measurements, it's best to stick to them.

With the wire stock flat, I start to file the design into the silver (see Image 3). Starting from one end and working the full length, I use a bastard-cut file. My file strokes start with the cutting edge of the file, which I dig into the silver. This makes one side of the cut deeper than the other, resulting in the tapered design. With the edge of the file digging into the corner of the square wire, I continue filing, favoring the deep edge of the cut and making sure that my cut is even, producing a triangle-shaped design. I take care not to cut beyond the center of the square wire on the top and the side.

IMAGE 4: *Use a square file (right) to start the file cuts, and a double half-round file (left) to control the next series of cuts and create the scalloped design.*

For the scalloped design cuff, I start my file cuts with an aggressive square file. This allows me to control the next series of cuts using a double half-round file (see Image 4), which has two radii on either side and is one of the most useful files I have in my tool set. The square file gives my double half-round file a notch to grab onto so that it doesn't skid as it removes the silver.

I file the scallops into the square wire all the way across the top of the wire and halfway down the edge of the wire, alternating the cuts so they are not cutting into each other.

I'm not specifying the layout, inches, millimeters, and ways to follow my measurements because all of that is design dependent. If your filing is not perfect, and your design is changing before your eyes, take a breath and keep at it. Do not give up. This is the difference between successful artists and the ones who are so worried about perfection that they never finish anything.

My filing technique differs from those of other instructors. I teach my students to file back and forth, telling them that, if they have a lot of time,

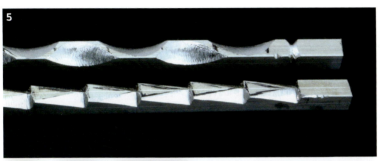

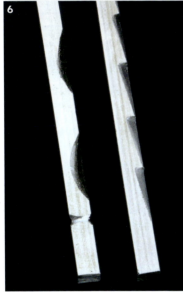

IMAGE 5: *Both wires after the initial cutting. The bottom wire shows how far down the sides were cut.*
IMAGE 6: *The left wire shows how the end can be modified to allow for finishing with a decorative pattern.*

they can file in one direction, but it's not necessary. I tell them to push into the cut and draw the file back along the same way without lifting it. This is much faster, and you will see results much sooner. I have found no disadvantages to this technique in 40 years of filing.

Image 5 shows my square wires with the initial cutting done. The bottom wire also shows how far I cut down the sides. The side cuts are even because I drew a line with my dividers to indicate the center of the wire.

Image 6 shows how to terminate the design. I don't like to just stop my design in the scalloped cuff. I like to play with the ends of the bracelet in a way that adds to the overall look and stops the central design.

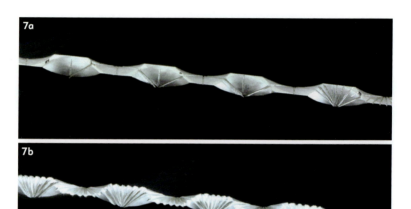

IMAGES 7a and 7b: *To complete the scalloped bracelet, make a layout in each scallop using a 2/0 saw blade. Image 7a shows the progression of strokes from left to right. In Image 8 (page 137), the scallops have all been cut, and the ends decorated.*

To complete the scalloped bracelet, I cut a fan-shaped design into the center of each scallop (see Images 7a and 7b). I start by making a layout in each scallop with a saw and a 2/0 saw blade. I estimate the centers of both the top and the bottom of each scallop and mark them with a shallow saw cut. The saw blade is convenient because you can see through the saw frame and make marks more accurately than with a file. From the center spots, I mark the farthest I'm going to cut the design on each side of the scallop. Then I fill in with more saw marks between the initial three marks. A file is useless here since the area is too small to measure and mark with a scriber or dividers. Instead, I must estimate these marks.

Once the marks are saw cut, I use a triangle needle file to make them wider and more defined, as well as to make the sides of the cuts rounder and deeper and to bring the cut up over the edge of the scallop.

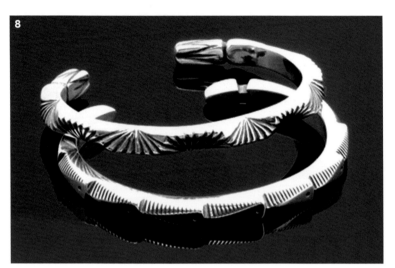

IMAGE 8: *The finished bracelets.*

Image 8 shows the finished bracelets. The scalloped cuff was finished on the ends with a series of cuts, starting with a shallow saw cut and finishing with triangle needle files. The lined triangle cuff was finished by making parallel lines on each filed-in triangle with a checkering file. As a final detail, I added a dot to the top of each triangle with an automatic center punch.

Once these cuffs are bent, their beauty comes out. The design's transformation is just amazing. Even the most dubious students have gasped in joy after bending the filed square wire into a cuff shape.

To finish these cuffs, I use liver of sulfur to patinate the recesses and polish off the top areas to a high shine.

For more information, see *The Complete Metalsmith* by Tim McCreight and *The Theory and Practice of Goldsmithing* by Dr. Erhard Brepohl.

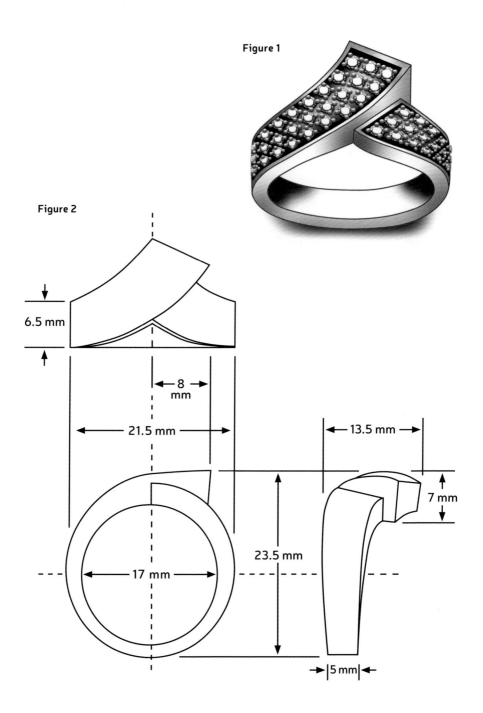

Wax CARVING

Lost-wax casting is a fundamental process in jewelry making. While CAD/CAM production has revolutionized the making of "wax" models, a basic understanding of 2-D design drawing, architectural break-out of 2-D, and transfer of dimensions to a 3-D format are still required of a designer/craftsperson.

How to Use This Project

When using this project for skill training, have apprentices start with an assignment of drawing a three-quarter view of a ring design (Figure 1, page 138).

Then have them break out the design into an architectural diagram of top, side, and edge views (Figure 2, page 138).

Have apprentices repeat the drawing process with more complex jewelry designs, using templates and measuring gauges until they gain competence in this process. Then move forward with transferring measurements and wax carving.

When using this technique to assess more intermediate skill levels, have

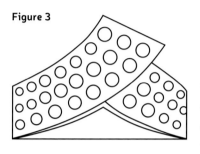

Figure 3

apprentices who have already demonstrated aptitude in drawing, begin with this very simple design (Figure 3) and time their progress to completion. An apprentice who has some skill at wax carving should take no more than three hours to carve this wax to specified dimensions. Allow another two to three hours of training with a master stone setter to complete the pavé stone layout with bead prongs.

If your company wants to hire for CAD/CAM assistance, the architectural diagram of top, side, and edge views can be imported into CAD software for further development. Have apprentices scan their diagrams and use the three views as background bitmaps to aid in creating the CAD model.

Skills:

- Hand drawing and architectural diagram
- Transferring from 2-D to 3-D
- Scribing, dividers and caliper use
- Precision measuring and marking
- Wax sawing and trimming

Materials:

- Wax ring tube

Tools:

- Drafting supplies
- Brass slide gauge
- Dividers
- Scribe
- Jeweler's saw frame with wax saw blades
- Wax files and hand files
- Flex-shaft
- Setting burs
- Ball burs
- Scrapers
- Calipers
- Reamer/ring tube sizer

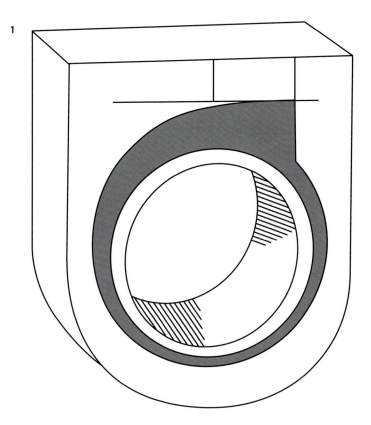

Wax Carving

1. Using a prepared wax ring tube, measure and cut a block to the required thickness (14 mm) that will accommodate the design.

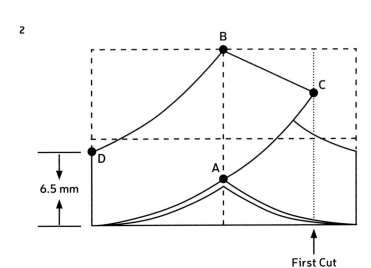

2. Use a reamer/ring tube sizer to enlarge the center hole to the required ring size (7). Measure, mark, and remove any extra height from the top and sides of the ring tube block, keeping it square and flat on top. Use calipers and dividers to measure and mark center lines on the top and sides. Painting white-out on the wax to reveal the scribed center lines will help with layout and transfer of measurements. Using the top view of the architectural diagram, plot out the significant points of the ring design onto the flat top of the ring tube block.

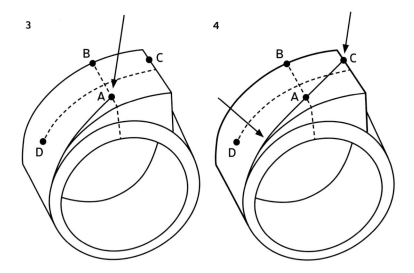

3. For this asymmetrical "sweep" design, the cleavage element is indicated by plotting point "A," which is established on the center line. The second plotting point, "B," is the end of the sweep; it is also established on the center line. To find the location of the third plotting point, "C," check the architectural diagram to get the measurement from the center line to that point.

4. Use dividers to scribe a straight line in from the edge of the ring tube block intersecting plotting point "C." This line will be the first cut to remove material for the design. Each time material is removed, reestablish the center lines, plotting points, and curve lines necessary to keep the design clear.

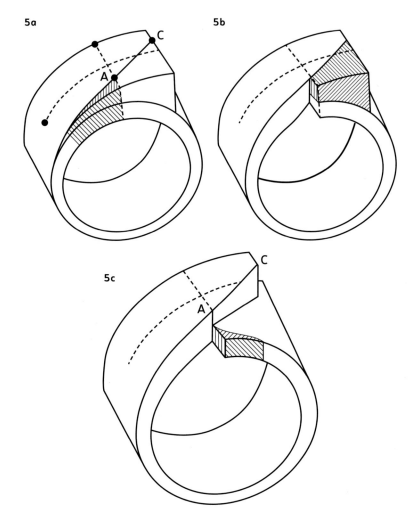

5. Continue to remove material as indicated in the illustrations.

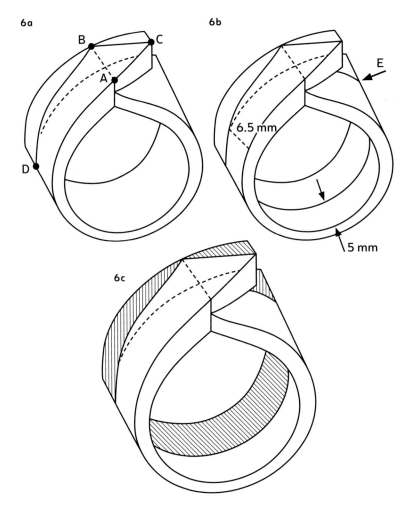

6. Scribe a line from plotting point "B" to point "C." Using dividers and measuring from plotting point "D," scribe a line around the shank of the ring to mark where additional material should be removed.

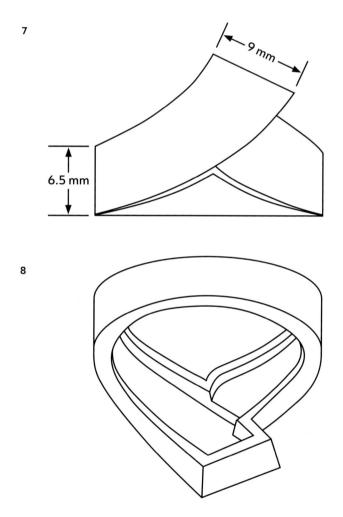

7. Check your measurements on the wax using calipers or a brass slide gauge.

8. Use ball burs and scrapers to hollow the underside of the ring, leaving a 1.5 mm frame on all edges.

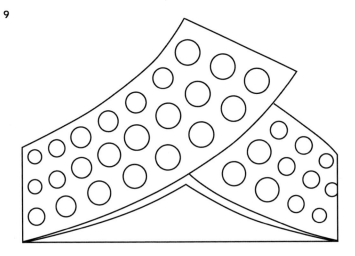

9

9. Work with a stone setter to lay out the pavé stone arrangement for the top of the ring. After drilling holes for each stone, use stone-setting burs in the appropriate millimeter sizes to cut beveled seats where each stone will be placed.

For more information on jewelry illustration, wax carving, and CAD design, I recommend *Jewelry Illustration* by Dominique Audette, *Jewelry Wax Modeling* by Adolfo Mattiello, and *Rhino for Jewelry* by Dana Buscaglia.

Rivet Capture
PENDANT

The use of rivets to join metal is a fundamental goldsmithing technique. Rivets are used to connect links in bracelets, hinges for watches and lockets, as well as in stone setting.

Using dividers and a brass slide gauge for planning a rivet capture setting is essential. Measuring and marking the metal for exact drill hole placement can make or break this style of setting. This project will illustrate how using these elemental measuring tools will help to make your work more precise.

Making a Rivet Capture Pendant

With this rivet capture pendant, spaced rivets will be used to provide a protective area for the gemstones girdle and culet. The spaced rivets will also serve as an area through which a chain can be threaded.

How to Use This Project

When using this project for skill training, you should have the apprentice

begin by practicing measuring and marking distances with the divider on sheet metal and tubing, as illustrated in the text. Use these scribed marks to practice sawing in straight, curved lines and turning corners with the saw blade. Have the apprentices familiarize themselves by using the leverage gauge to measure when cutting multiple matching small parts.

When using this technique to assess more intermediate skill levels, have apprentices plan for material use and complete this simple project within a set time period of 8-10 hours. Check for precision of tubing lengths, drill-hole placement, overall balance of proportions, clean rivet heads, and finish. Use this pendant as the culmination project when grouping techniques such as measuring and marking methods, jeweler's saw training, polishing training, and rivet making.

Skills:
- Precise measuring and marking
- Cutting and fitting small components
- Setting bur use
- Rivet making and multiple-rivet setting
- Stone setting

Materials:
- Faceted gemstone
- 20-gauge sterling sheet, roll-printed is optional
- 16-gauge round sterling wire
- Tubing to fit snugly over the wire

Tools:
- Awl
- Brass slide gauge
- Bench anvil or block
- Bench vise
- Burs: hart bur or setting bur
- Circle cutter (optional)
- Dividers
- Flex-shaft
- Hammer for riveting: this can be a cross-peen or finely finished ball-peen hammer
- Hand files: various cuts
- Hydraulic press (optional)
- Jeweler's saw with saw blades
- Pliers: round/needle nose
- Tube cutting jig (optional)
- Circle template
- #56 drill bit
- Sandpaper

Steps to Making a Rivet Capture Pendant

1. Select a gemstone for setting and an outer shape for the pendant. For this project, I have selected a cushion-cut, concave-faceted lemon quartz. To accent the cushion shape, set the gemstone on point in a round opening. Using the size of the gemstone, proportion the size of your pendant. Saw out three identical panels in 20-gauge metal. File and sand the edges of the panels so the shapes match. Two of the panels will be used to create the rivet capture for the gemstone, while the third panel will serve as a guard on the back of the pendant to keep the culet of the gemstone safe.

2. To mark precise measurements with the dividers and the brass slide gauge, open the dividers to the measurement as indicated on the brass slide gauge. I recommend using the millimeter measurements because they are smaller increments than sixteenths of an inch.

3. To mark each metal panel with the same measurement, use one edge of a metal panel as a guide, hooking a leg of the dividers against that edge, and drag the other leg of the divider along the interior of the metal panel to scribe a line.

4. The first set of scribed lines in this project will mark where the opening for the gemstone will be cut. Gemstone openings are only necessary in the top and the middle panels. Use the spot where the scribed lines intersect to establish guidelines on the panels, and then use a circle template to mark where the gemstone opening will be cut. The opening for the gemstone can be the same shape as the gemstone, or it can accent the stone by being open around parts of the stone. The lemon quartz in this project is 14 mm point to point. The opening cut for this gemstone is a 13 mm circle. TIP: Cut the opening for the gemstone with a circle cutter in the hydraulic press. Using a hydraulic press with a circle cutter will cut the circles cleanly, keep the tool exactly where you have placed it on the metal, and extend the life of your circle cutter.

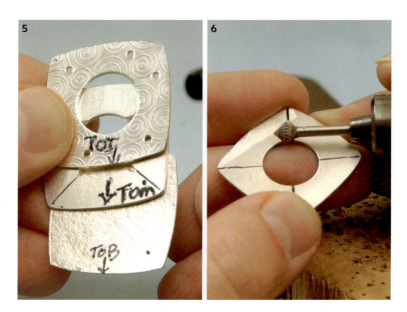

5. Mark the panels with a permanent marker to indicate the top of the top panel (ToT), the top of the middle one (ToM), and the top of the bottom panel (ToB). This will help to complete the project successfully.

6. Viewing the gemstone openings like the face of a clock, use the brass slide gauge to mark the openings where you will cut the seats for setting at noon, three, six, and nine o'clock on the back of the top panel and on the top of the middle panel. Then use a 45-degree hart bur to cut "V" notches.

7. Refine the notches with the edge of a square key file.

8. Place the gemstone into the notches between the top and middle panels to check the seats. If the gemstone's girdle is too thick for the panels to sit level and flush, you may need to measure and cut tube spacers to place on the rivet wires. These small tube spacers will hold the panels at an appropriate distance to secure the gemstone without breaking or chipping its facets. With the gemstone between the top and middle panels, use the brass slide gauge to estimate how far the back panel will need to be from the middle panel for the culet to be protected. This estimate will give you an indication of how long the pieces of tubing will need to be for the long tube spacers.

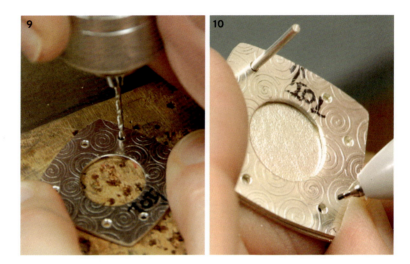

9. Scribe a second set of lines on the back of the top panel. Place this second set of scribed lines between the opening for the gemstone and the outside edge of the panel. This second set of scribed lines will act as a guide for placing and drilling all the rivet holes at an equal distance from the outer edge of the pendant. The trick to the multiple-rivet technique this setting requires is to drill all the holes on only one panel. I cannot stress this enough—drill only the top panel. As the rivets will be made from 16-gauge wire, I use #56 drill bit to drill holes on the top panel only.

10. With the gemstone in place, align the openings of the top and middle panels. Then, using the top panel as a guide, mark through a single drill hole onto the middle panel with a fine-tip permanent marker. Use the top panel as a guide to mark the bottom panel as well.

11. Dimple and drill only one hole in the middle and bottom panel and thread a rivet wire through all three panels. Do not set the rivet. Align all three panels using the single rivet wire to register the panels. Continuing to use the top panel as a guide, select the hole opposite to the rivet and drill through the middle and bottom panels. Thread another rivet wire through that hole, but do not set the rivet.

12. Flare one end of a 1-inch length of wire in a bench vise to create the rivet wires. Repeat the process of threading rivet wires into each drilled hole before you drill the next. This process will keep your holes and panels registered and aligned until you are ready to set the rivets. The unset rivets will hold the panels together as you file and sand all the outer edges. As you separate the panels, mark each one with an arrow to indicate its correct alignment. Place the arrow on each panel near the spot where you have marked the panel with ToT, ToM, and ToB. Again, this alignment marking will be necessary to completing the project successfully.

13. Based on your earlier measurements use the dividers to mark identical lengths of tubing for each rivet. [Note: Master goldsmiths should instruct apprentices in proper tube-cutting techniques.]

14. After the tubing has been cut, file and sand the ends of each piece to make sure they are level. Hold the tube with your round-nose pliers and feed it up from under the bench pin. This way, you can use the flat top of your bench pin to provide a level surface for filing or sanding the tube end. Slanted tube ends or tubing of unequal lengths will result in an uneven pendant and may jeopardize the stability of the gemstone setting. When the tubes are level, check them with the leverage gauge to make sure they are all the same length.

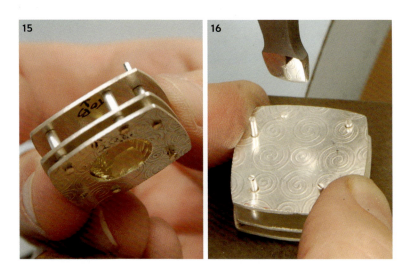

15. Once you have prepared and pre-polished all the parts, begin assembling the pendant. Use the alignment arrows to line up all the panels. Denatured alcohol on a cotton swab can be used to remove the permanent marker as you assemble the parts. With the gemstone and spacer tubes in place, begin to trim the rivet wires with a flush cutter and set the rivets.

16. Place a layer or two of masking tape over the table of the gemstone to protect it during the riveting process. Loosely set each rivet so that it will not come out. Then proceed to tighten each rivet in opposition by lightly tightening one rivet and then tightening the rivet opposite it. This way, the gemstone setting is tightened around the stone evenly, and pressure is not brought down onto the gemstone from any one direction to cause a stress fracture. Once all the rivets are set, finish polishing all the edges with either a buffing wheel or fine sand papers.

For additional information, see *Creative Stonesetting* by John Cogswell and *The Complete Metalsmith* by Tim McCreight.

Boudoir Medicine Receptical by Nanz Aalund
2015 Saul Bell Award Finalist

Slot-in-Slot
CONSTRUCTION

Slot-in-slot construction has been used throughout jewelry-making history. The technique has been found in pieces dating back over 7,000 years. In recent times with the advent of mass-produced/commercially available heads for stone setting, this technique has become overlooked in goldsmith training. The most prominent version of this technique is the classic Tiffany engagement ring with a four- or six-prong head. The pronged head is made using this technique, and it can be adapted for many creative purposes.

How to Use This Project

For training and assessment, use CZs or plastic rhinestones for practice gemstone setting. I recommend using 18-gauge copper or brass since the edges of the metal holding the gemstone will be visible. Thinner gauges can be used, but they may look flimsy.

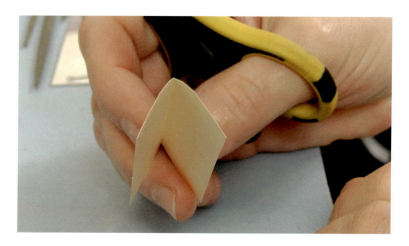

Using This Project for Skill Training

Have the apprentice start with larger stones to fabricate larger heads. Repeat the exercise, working toward smaller and smaller dimensions. Have the apprentice create their own designs out of heavy construction paper or card stock.

This is very inexpensive. Once the apprentice has absorbed how the process works with paper, have them replicate it in metal. Designing larger style settings with interior openings, as shown below, also trains for precision piercing skills and can be grouped with jeweler's saw training.

Using This Technique to Assess Skill Levels

Have apprentices start with the smallest stones they feel competent using to fabricate a head and set the stone. Keep track of how long they take and how well the sample turns out.

Skills:
- Precise measuring and marking
- Scoring and folding for duplication
- Precision sawing/piercing
- Fitting small elements
- Stone setting

Materials:
- Card stock
- 11-14 mm cushion-cut gemstone
- 20-gauge sheet stock (3 x 3 inches)
- 18-gauge wire (2 inches)
- Hard and medium solder

Tools:
- Scissors
- Glue stick
- Jeweler's saw frame and 2/0 blades
- Bench pin
- Bench vice
- Triangular hand file (2 cut)
- Separating discs (optional)
- 45-degree hart bur/setting bur
- Flex-shaft
- Soldering station
- Polishing materials
- Parallel pliers with nylon jaw liner
- Dividers
- Rawhide mallet
- Flat needle file
- Triangular needle file

Steps to Making a Slot-in-Slot Setting

1. Measure the design drawing or use a paper pattern to get the correct width for the sheet stock. To ensure that the sheet metal is of the correct size for this project, measure the height of the design and double that measurement.

2. Use your dividers to mark the center line of the sheet stock.

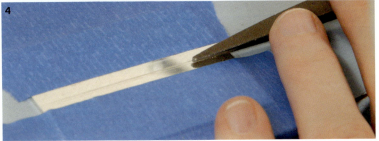

3. To make sure the two pieces of the setting are identical, use a score-and-fold technique. Before scoring, the master goldsmith should guide the apprentice in determining whether the metal's temper is half-hard; if it has been milled to full work-hardened, it will require annealing. To start the score line, you can use a 45-degree hart bur or a separating disc with a flex-shaft. These discs can shatter, so go slowly and wear safety glasses.

4. With the edge of a triangular hand file, file a V-groove approximately three-quarters through the depth of the gauge on a center line perpendicular to the width.

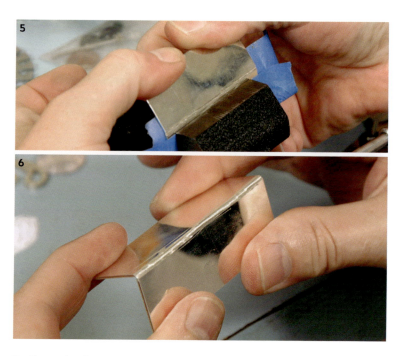

5. Clamp the sheet stock in a bench vise to fold the height of the sheet in half.

6. Make sure the filed V-groove is on the exterior of the fold. Fold the two halves of the metal sheet completely back and use a rawhide mallet to tamp the folded piece flat. File the open edges of the folded piece even and straight, as many of the rest of your measurements will depend on these edges being straight.

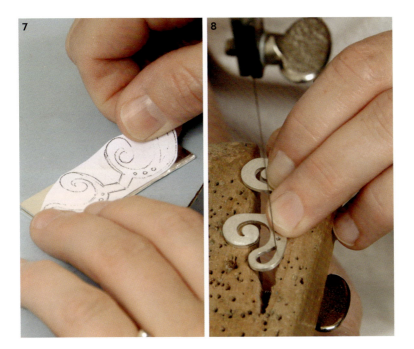

7. Apply a paper pattern to the folded metal piece and pierce out the design. Make sure not to saw away the area where the fold is holding the panels together.

8. Saw close to the outside of your marked lines and then file precisely up to the marked line. Continue to work on the piece by drilling and sawing any internal cuts and then filing and sanding all edges.

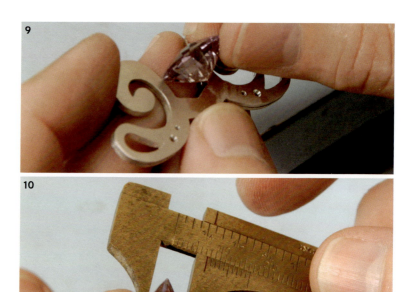

9. Check the fit of the gemstone in the opening where the seat will be cut. The tricky part of this style of setting is that you need to make sure the gemstone will fit before it is assembled.

10. For this setting, you will be filing several notches in the panels at specific placements—one to set the gemstone and another for a support ring under the gemstone, which is called an "under bezel." Measure the depth of the gemstone to determine exactly where these notches should be placed.

11. Use a 45-degree setting bur or a triangular needle file to make the notches. For extra strength, use 18-gauge round wire for the under bezel. Make the under bezel 1 mm smaller than the diameter of the gemstone. When the folded metal piece is completely pierced and finished, remove the top folded area. Now you will have two separate but identical panels.

12. Mark and cut a slot in the center of one panel going from the bottom of the panel to halfway up the base.

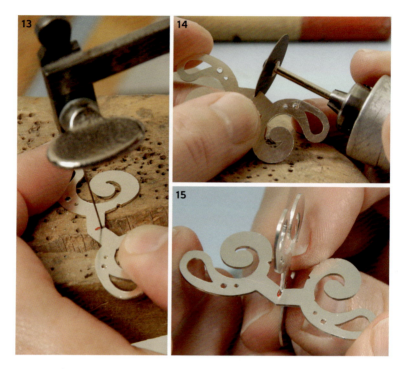

13. On the second panel, mark and cut another slot in the center of the panel under where the stone will be set and going about halfway down. Both slots should be as wide as the gauge of the metal, but no wider.

14. Use a separating disc or flat needle files to trim the slots. Be careful because too wide of a slot will allow the panels to flop around, making a sloppy setting.

15. Pre-polish the panels, removing scratches and file marks. Slide the slots into each other so that the panels are perpendicular. This fitting should be tight.

16. Solder the panels at the center join with hard solder. Fit the under bezel into the lower notches and solder with medium silver solder.

17. Bring the panels back up to a bright polish with felt buffs and rouge.

18. Enlarge the notches for the gemstone seat with a 45-degree setting bur or a needle file.

19. Use parallel pliers with nylon jaw liners to gently pull the panels back above the stone seats. This will open the setting to allow the gemstone to be slipped into place.

20. Using the parallel pliers with the nylon jaw liners, straighten the top section of each panel until the stone is set tightly.

21. The final result.

For additonal information, see *Creative Stonesetting* by John Cogswell and *Professional Jewelry Making* by Alan Revere.

"The Soroya" Necklace by Jose Lins
2013 Saul Bell Emerging Jewelry Artist Award

Introductory
FILIGREE BEAD

Completion of fine soldering procedures without unintentional melting is a primary skill every goldsmith or jeweler must master. Using a soldering pick to transport tiny amounts of solder from the soldering block to the join site is an elemental soldering skill for professional jewelry craftspeople. Mastering these techniques is necessary for advanced, efficient jewelry fabrication. I developed this project as an exercise for gaining mastery of the advanced skills of torch control and pick soldering technique. An added advantage to this project is the technique of applying binding wire to hold the pieces together during the final assembly.

How to Use This Project

When using this project for skill training, group it with rolling mill, annealing, and draw-plate use training for progressive skill development. Have apprentices practice pouring ingots of sterling silver and rolling out and drawing down those ingots to various gauges and shapes of wire. Once they have successfully completed making the silver wire for this project, they can move on to brass or nickel wire to make several of these coiled "Xs." Have them start with heavier gauges of wire and progress to finer ones. Use the three silver solders of hard, medium, and easy to complete a single bead. After the apprentices have completed several beads in the finer gauges of brass or nickel, have them progress to the silver wire they had drawn down.

When using this project to assess more intermediate skill levels, have the apprentice complete the group of skills to mill the wire and make several beads in silver, progressing to ever finer wire and smaller beads. To assess competence, check beads for melted tips, clean joins, tool marks, and smooth wire curls.

Skills:

- Wire drawing and bending
- Pliers use
- Precision soldering
- Dapping
- Binding wire use

Materials:

- 18-gauge copper or silver wire
- 20-gauge steel binding wire

Tools:

- Round-nose pliers
- Wire cutters
- Chasing hammer
- Rawhide mallet
- Parallel pliers with nylon jaws
- Dapping block with dapping punches
- Soldering equipment
- Sandpapers
- Hand files
- Ring or bezel mandrel

Instructions for a Standard-Size Bead

1. Cut two 2-inch (51 mm) pieces of 18-gauge (1 mm) round wire.

2. Cross the wires at the center of each so they make an X with the wires at right angles to each other. With a flat hammer face, tap the center of the X to score both wires at that point. Solder the wires together at the center point with hard solder. Repeat for the second X. Measure each wire to make sure each leg of the X is 1 inch long.

3. Use a ball-peen hammer face to slightly flatten the ends of each wire. File and sand the flattened wire tips.

4. Use round-nose pliers to start each spiral. Hold the flattened wire end with the tip of the pliers while rolling the wire around the pliers' nose. Hold the center of the X while coiling the wires to make sure you have a firm grip.

5. Switch to a nylon-jawed parallel pliers, holding the start of the coil in the jaw while pushing the wire with your thumb to continue evenly rolling the coil.

6. Using medium solder, join the outer edges of the coils to each other. (The head of one coil should be soldered to the back of the other.) This will hold the coils in place while doming them. Repeat for the second coiled X.

7. Place the coiled Xs into the dapping block and press with a dap to dome. Start in a larger hemisphere, progressing to smaller hemispheres on the block.

8. Use a bit of tape to hold the back of the domed X while sanding it to flatten spots on the coils to assemble them. Make a ring from 16-gauge square wire to a diameter that will fit both domed, coiled Xs. To get the exact length of square wire to use, find the diameter in millimeters of the coiled and domed X, add the thickness of the square wire in millimeters, and multiply the total by Pi. Solder the ring closed with hard solder. Round out the ring on a ring or bezel mandrel.

9. Use steel binding wire in 20-gauge to hold the three pieces of the bead together.

10. Solder the coiled and domed Xs onto the ring with easy solder. Use pick soldering technique to apply small balls of easy solder to each of the joins. Make sure you remove all steel binding wire before placing the bead into the pickle. For an extra level of difficulty, use easy silver solder to solder jump rings to the bead, or remove the center band for a more delicate bead.

For more information, see *Silver Threads: Making Filigree Jewelry* by Jean Rhodes-Moen and *Russian Filigree* (DVD) by Victoria Lansford.

Apprenticeship
SUCCESS STORY

SAM PATANIA
Owner, Patania's Sterling Silver Originals, Tucson, Arizona

How old were you when you started making jewelry/metals?
I was 15 years old when I started making jewelry. My high school gave me credit to take an art class from my father [who at the time was running the family's jewelry studio, the Thunderbird Shop, in Tucson, Arizona]. My route was purely through my father who himself had apprenticed under his father. I was fortunate to have a master craftsman as a father and the desire to stick with it. He had me start by

making a wire sculpture with baling wire, small scale, no larger than 4 inches high. It got my brain going in 3-D. I have never been able to draw to my satisfaction, so starting out working in 3-D was fortunate.

What kind of training did you receive or seek?

I received an apprenticeship from my father, which lasted 10 years. I was not encouraged to design during that time, just produce whatever my dad asked for and the business required. I started with very basic projects and progressed into a journeyman silversmith. It was an old-fashioned type of training, and I did whatever the business needed as far as cleaning, merchandising, selling, packaging and shipping, errands, maintenance, tool making, customer service, delivery, as well as making jewelry.

In which techniques have you been trained?

I trained in silversmithing in a southwestern style, which can be described as "get it done." I was taught how to use bent nails to set stones, and work with all types of inherited handmade tools that were not commercially available.

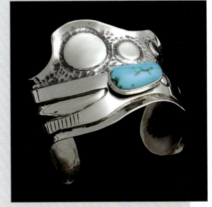

I would make bezels, trace templates to hand-saw all the designs given to me, and form all kinds of jewelry. I learned how to polish to a high shine and use liver of sulfur.

My dad taught me some repoussé and forging, which I [continued to explore] on my own. Neither was usual in our businesses inventory. My dad also taught me a bit of sand casting, and I went on to explore production lost-wax casting.

I learned platinumsmithing on my own and taught myself to set stones in gold prongs as well. Mike Croft at the University of Arizona metals department taught me how to cast and use the mokume gane process.

Have you taken on an apprentice?

I have taken on many apprentices. Some came from California, one arrived from England, and most were from the Tucson area. A number of the many apprentices I employed were affiliated with schools; some just wanted to learn from me for short periods of time (two to three months). I currently employ both my son and my daughter as apprentices. I do this to teach what I have learned.

Apprenticeship
SUCCESS STORY

RONDA CORYELL
Owner, Ronda Coryell Designs, Albuquerque, New Mexico

How old were you when you started making jewelry/metals?
I had studied metals at Ohio State University (OSU) in my 20s, but I was 40 years old before I started doing metals as a career. There was an ad in the newspaper for a bench jeweler, and I went in to apply. I had never fixed anything; I mostly carved waxes and did casting in college. The shop owner took me to a wax bench and said, "Make something." I had not carved a wax in 15 years and I was so nervous, I broke the first one. I quickly carved another, and he hired me as a model maker.

Did you seek other master craftsmen to apprentice with?
At that first job, I had five master jewelers teaching me what I needed to know to make my ideas work. Each jeweler had a different way of doing things, so it was quite an education.

In which techniques were you trained?
Within two years, I opened my own jewelry store and started going to workshops to study specific techniques. I loved the challenge of hard-to-duplicate pieces, so I picked the best in the area to study under. John Cogswell for silversmithing (vessels and flatware), Heikki Seppa and Michael Good (for anticlastic metalsmithing), Jean Stark (for 22k gold granulation), among many others. High-karat gold granulation became my main focus. I never wanted to be limited by my knowledge, so I became a fourth-level Jewelers of America (JA) Master Bench Jeweler.

Did you have help to start your business?
After graduating from OSU, I did not. I went into stained-glass work for 14 years, doing major commissions. My last project was a Catholic church that took two years to complete. But when I started my own jewelry store I did have a mentor who helped me out. I was very lucky to have his help.

Have you trained any apprentices?

Apprenticeships are a way of sharing the knowledge. If someone can find a candidate to train—a young person in high school or college or an older person at retirement age—that person can be trained to do things your way. My entire goal  now is to give jewelry-making information to as many students as possible. One of the reasons I teach and am a mentor is that I always feel pride in helping my students achieve their goals. Belle Brooke Barer of Belle Brooke Designs in Santa Fe, New Mexico, someone that I regard as a colleague, is a former student I mentored. Dan Sweiterman from Austin, Texas, is now a master jeweler. I still hear from students who were not just apprentices, but have become like my children. And a parent is always proud of their children.

CHAPTER 7

Advice FOR THOSE BEGINNING THEIR JEWELRY CAREERS

Editor's note: While this guide is primarily directed toward shop owners interesting in establishing apprenticeships, apprentices should also read its chapters. In doing so, they will have a better understanding of the jewelry business owner's goals and challenges in taking on an apprentice. The guide will also help apprentices to learn what potential employers need from them, and to recognize that no matter their background—whether they are an advanced graduate from the most prestigious trade school or a high school student with only a few hundred hours of experience—they will need to learn more. Some of that learning will come from the apprenticeship, but it won't end there: Learning is a lifelong journey, and the committed apprentice can look toward various schools, workshops, and training programs to help them on that journey toward professional success.

In the following conversation, the guide's author, Nanz Aalund, and its consulting editor, Charles Lewton-Brain, discuss the ways in which jewelers can better learn their craft. They also talk about the importance of jewelry to the *human experience—a foundation that any jeweler should know about and take to heart.*

The Cultural Role Played by Jewelry

CL-B: Jewelry is very important to human beings. All peoples self-decorate in some manner. The oldest evidence of human consciousness was thought to be 40,000 years ago, then it was changed to 70,000 years ago, and now it is believed to have occurred over 100,000 years ago. And the evidence of that consciousness is jewelry—specifically, beads. It's true that organic materials do not last, but stone and fossilized shell beads do. Some archaeologists say that self-decoration helped to drive human consciousness, of which these beads are evidence.

NA: Yes, when I read of the Blombos Cave archaeological discovery in South Africa, Prof. Christopher Stuart Henshilwood of the University of Bergen, Norway, who led the exploration, was quoted in the Associated Press as saying, "Beads are a serious matter in traditional societies, providing identification by gender, age, social class, and ethnic group." This indicates that beads and self-decoration with them are evidence of the early origins of modern human behavior and the ability to use language, which would have been essential for "sharing and transmitting the symbolic meaning of the beads … within and beyond the group." Supporting that statement, Alison Brooks, an anthropology professor at The George Washington University in Washington, DC, is also quoted in the Associated Press, citing these ancient beads as "an unequivocal argument that people are employing symbols to signify who they are."

CL-B: It's fascinating when you consider that the use of jewelry as a self-identifier is an ancient act and has been around so long that the need to wear it could almost be considered genetic. This paradigm offers a way to understand why cultures separated by vast expanses of time and geography all seem to ascribe similar symbolic meanings to precious metals and gemstones.

How Does One Learn to Be a Jeweler?

CL-B: This is a question that people of various ages ask me. Some are teenagers who want to be jewelers, some are young professionals or mature individuals making life-changing choices, and some are hobbyists who find they want to get more serious.

NA: The jewelry field today is huge. There are so many places in its spectrum where one can choose to work, to make a career, and to build a creative life. It is so complex and detailed that there is no way a single individual could ever learn it all, or gain the different skills needed to operate in all its facets. [*pun intended*]

CL-B: And that is what makes being a jeweler so interesting. One can be a goldsmith, art/craft jeweler, store owner, designer/maker, setter, digital or hand wax model maker, gemologist, gemstone/diamond dealer, and so on.

How you learn jewelry skills differs by culture. In some cultures, including our own until recently, jewelry making was kept a great secret, to be passed on only to trusted family members. In Mexico, where there is a secret vocabulary for shopping at a jewelry or metals supplier (yellow is gold, white is silver), if you don't know the words you don't get to buy. The Ganoksin Project (*ganoksin.com*), which I co-founded with Dr. Hanuman Aspler [in 1995-96], addressed this secrecy head-on and went some way toward loosening those boundaries.

NA: In some ways, there are as many paths to becoming a jeweler as there are jewelry techniques. Many people have said to me that they are "self-taught," but really they mean that they sought out specific teachers and then practiced solo. Self-directed learning like this can be difficult to do, as the willpower required is high, yet many successful individuals in our field cite this as their pathway.

CL-B: For those who want to take this path, there are numerous books, lots of videos, and quite a bit of information online. It's encouraging that there's so much more access to technical education: YouTube videos, online workshops, DVDs, and interactive webinars in many jewelry techniques. The archives of Ganoksin offer a great technical resource for jewelry makers at all levels.

NA: I agree, there are more books and technical manuals available now for jewelry manufacturing than ever before, with excellent illustrations. Many of those books are referenced in the projects of this book. However, with the abundance of hobby-craft practitioners, students will want to research the credentials of the authors to make sure they're getting technically solid and professional instruction.

CL-B: That is important. Also, it is best to plan a program of study based on what facet of the jewelry world you want to specialize in, what you want your day to look like five years from now, and what you think you want from this path. The fastest route is to talk to someone who is doing what you think you want to do and ask them how they got to where they are.

NA: Concentrating on the information and skills that make the most sense in accomplishing one's goals is a viable path. A combination of self-directed study and short courses can also be effective.

CL-B: A good eight- to ten-week evening course can be an excellent introduction to the field. Well-equipped community-based schools, craft centers, and small metals studios with teaching spaces are popping up across the U.S., and some provide very good introductory programs.

NA: And some programs bring in master artists such as yourself to teach intensive workshops. These workshops also serve to upgrade skill sets and further the education of established makers in the field, so they can provide a resource for industry networking.

CL-B: Precisely, workshops are especially helpful to find and meet politely with the people who are doing what it is you think you want to do.

NA: If students can find one or more mentors, would you recommend they should try volunteering to work for a mentor to gain skills? When I was a novice, this path worked for me.

CL-B: Yes, volunteering your way in the door is an excellent way in. If you can identify which part of the jewelry making field you want to specialize in, then you can craft an efficient path to where you want to be. This may even present opportunities that reduce the time individuals spend to reach their goals.

Opportunities Offered by Degree Programs

NA: There are several state technical schools that teach jewelry making. These state-supported vocationally oriented programs are usually more affordable [than college or university programs]; in some cases, they cost less than a couple of thousand dollars a year. Some, like the Texas Institute for Jewelry Technology in Paris, Texas, teach to the Jewelers of America [JA] Bench Professional Certification tests.

There are also many colleges and universities that have jewelry/metals programs—although, in the United States, this number is dwindling or reduced to a single-professor department. Still, I strongly feel that the research-driven, creative, university/college metals programs offer the greatest opportunity for becoming highly skilled in complex problem solving. This is a sought-after and necessary skill that trade schools, although they excel in technical skills, seem to overlook. It is the mental flexibility of an adept problem solver that makes for the most creative goldsmith. At least this has proven true in my experience.

CL-B: In support of what you're saying, I had a student once, in an art college where I taught, who really wanted to be a goldsmith. He was technically excellent, but he became impatient with the writing courses and wide-ranging techniques we taught. I convinced him to stay until the end of his third year, when he left to work as a goldsmith at a high-end shop. Several years later I got a letter from him, expressing his gratitude for the art college experience. He said he knew far more than most others in the trade, could find technical solutions for problems others could not solve, and in general had benefited extraordinarily from the experience.

Opportunities Offered by Private and Technical Programs

CL-B: There are also a number of excellent private schools. Aimed at goldsmithing, gem setting, engraving, and digital and hand wax carving, they have solid jewelry-industry–oriented training programs and good equipment. Some have curriculum geared toward the JA bench certification tests and offer programs ranging from intensive three-day workshops to several months of advanced skill training.

NA: Here again it is important for jewelry students to do research when selecting a program at a private school or university, to make sure the techniques being offered will be beneficial their potential career path. Many different schools are recognized for excellence within the jewelry industry and their graduates are sought after. My advise is always to be open to as many educational opportunities as possible to stretch your skill sets.

*Editor's Note: The BEaJEWELER website (*beajeweler.com*) has a searchable online guide to schools that offer a range of programs in jewelry making and design.*

Apprenticeship SUCCESS STORY

NANZ AALUND
Owner, Nanz Aalund Art Jewelry, Poulsbo, Washington

How old were you when you started making jewelry/metals?
Like the majority of goldsmiths I have met, I officially began making jewelry around the age of 15 with the help of a high school art teacher. As an undiagnosed dyslexic, I was not college bound due to my assessment scores in high school. Yet my first-ever official art teacher saw something in my aptitude for color theory, my patience with challenging processes, and my willingness to try again and again and

again. She put a torch in my hand, and I was hooked. She connected with me long after graduation, and when she saw that I was floundering, she helped me get accepted to a state university's metals program.

Once I was accepted to the university based on the strength of my early portfolio, there were still the challenges of the academic world. But my high school art teacher took me to the doorstep of my future and happily opened the door. And I bless her for that.

What kind of training did you receive or seek? Describe your route into the jewelry business.
Following high school, I served a three-year apprenticeship with a small mom-and-pop jewelry store in the northern suburbs of Chicago. It was mostly sweeping floors and cleaning toilets, but they did eventually teach me how to refine gold from scraps and sweeps. As the apprenticeship progressed, I learned to mill sizing stock, draw wire, and process castings. From books and workshops, I learned to fabricate with silver and carve wax models.

Was there a jewelers' union you had to join? Would having one have helped?
During my bachelor's degree studies, the metals department would bring in speakers from the Chicago area to tell us about the jewelry business. I heard stories about a jewelers' union in the jewelry district of downtown Chicago, and about the fact that some of the "guild" shops or high-end jewelers in the more prestigious suburbs hired "union men." But because of my gender, I was never offered work as a goldsmith in the Chicago area.

After receiving a BFA in metals and jewelry design from Northern Illinois University, I relocated to Seattle and was hired by Meyer Bros. Jewelry Manufacturer, a non-union shop at the time. A few years later, while working for a "guild-trade" shop, two retired union members assisted me in completing my journeyman papers through the last vestiges of the San Francisco Jewelers' Union. Six months and $1,500 later, I had journeyman status in a union that, sadly, no longer existed. But I had completed three master works in gold- and platinumsmithing, which taught me so many valuable techniques and skills.

I do believe a union for goldsmiths would be beneficial for training, credibility, accountability, quality standards, and maybe even collective insurance plans.

Did you seek a master craftsman to apprentice with?

Yes, throughout my career, I have sought out different master craftsmen and women to work with and learn from. While living in Germany, I was fortunate enough to be hired under-the-table to assist a master of military regalia. I took workshops with Alan Revere and other master craftsmen who taught at the Revere Academy in San Francisco. Finally, after 20 years as an award-winning goldsmith and jewelry designer in the jewelry industry, I undertook the challenge of a master's degree in fine art/metals. There again I felt as though I was apprenticing myself, but this time it was under the great American jewelry artist, Mary Lee Hu.

In which techniques were you trained?

Professionally, I have been trained in refining, alloying, casting, wax carving, master model fabrication, production manufacturing, gold and platinum fabrication, and stone setting. Through academia, I have been trained in the advanced silversmithing techniques of spinning, hydraulic press, laser welding and cutting, rapid prototyping/CAD-CAM, and design and educational techniques. Through workshops, I have learned keum-boo, lathe work, fold-forming, repoussé, and chasing.

Have you taken on an apprentice?

I began teaching at the Art Institute of Seattle in 2000 as a response to the lack of beneficial jewelry skill training in the trade. Shortly thereafter I was offered the teaching scholarship and artist-in-residency at the University of Washington, where I was able to work with hundreds of eager students. In recent years, I have mentored a couple of apprentices through a local government youth outreach program. I am very proud that several of my former students have achieved national recognition through jewelry industry design awards. But what is the most rewarding is sharing a passion for the craft.

Addendum:
A JEWELER'S VOCABULARY

This list includes some common terms with which apprentices should be familiar.

Acrylic Resin: A glassy thermoplastic used for cast and molded items; it comes in many colors and has been used in a wide variety of jewelry forms since the 1920s.

Agate: A variety of quartz, which includes chalcedony, sardonyx, carnelian, chrysoprase, and onyx. These translucent, porous stones have a waxlike luster.

Alloy: A mixture of two or more metals to make the predominant metal more durable.

Aluminum: A bluish, silver-white metallic element discovered in 1812. It is the most abundant metal in the Earth's crust. In the early 20th century, artists in the Arts and Crafts movement used it for jewelry.

Annealing: The process of relieving work stress within metal by heating it. Some metals require quenching, while others respond better to air-cooling.

Anodizing: The process of changing the surface color of a metal by using an electrical current. Most commonly used on aluminum and titanium.

Art Deco: A design style that originated in the 1920s as a reaction to Art Nouveau and gained prominence during the 1930s. Characterized by rectilinear forms, symmetry, and repetitive geometric patterns.

Art Nouveau: A design style that was prevalent between 1890 and 1910; it is characterized by flowing lines, intertwined flora and fauna, the feminine form, and asymmetry.

Arts and Crafts: A movement that thrived between 1888 and 1915. It revolted against expensive materials and industrial processes, valuing natural designs and a handcrafted art aesthetic.

Baguette: A long, narrow, rectangular cut for precious gems, such as diamonds.

Bail: The loop or ring at the top of a pendant by which it hangs.

Ball Peen: The spherical working end of a forming hammer.

Bench Jeweler: An artisan who has received training to work hands-on with jewelry tools and materials, and understands the processes necessary to create or repair jewelry.

Bench Pin: A wooden extension of the jeweler's bench upon which sawing, filing, and forming are done.

Bezel: A thin strip of metal formed to surround a stone, then pressed in and down on the stone to secure it in place.

Binding Wire: A soft iron or steel wire used to hold objects together and in place during soldering.

Brass: An alloy of copper and zinc.

Briolette: A teardrop-shaped gemstone cut with facets completely around the stone.

Burnish: To hand or machine polish a metal surface by rubbing it with a polished metal or stone tool called a burnisher.

Buffing: The final stage of creating a high polish. It can be done with machines or by hand.

CAD/CAM: Computer-aided design and computer-aided manufacturing.

Carat: A unit of weight used to measure gemstones. Originally determined by the weight of a carob seed.

Cabochon: A stone that has a smooth, rounded surface.

Casting: A process of creating metal objects by pouring molten metal into a hollow form made from sand, cuttlefish, or plaster.

Chasing: A process of embossing, adding fine detail or texture to the surface of sheet metal through the use of steel punches and hammer. (Also see the entry on Repoussé.)

Claw/Crown Setting: A symmetrical prong setting that resembles a claw or a small crown and is used to hold faceted gemstones. Also known as a "head."

Copper: A malleable, red-colored base metal. Popular for its versatility and low cost.

Cuttlefish: A marine animal whose porous white skeleton is used as a mold in one kind of direct casting.

Die: A metal form into which sheet metal is pushed for forming or cutting.

Dapping Block: A steel tool with round hemispherical depressions used to form domes. The steel rods with matching domes on the ends are called dapping punches, which are also available in wood to protect surface detail.

Draw Plate: A plate of hardened steel with funnel-shaped holes of diminishing size used to reduce wire in diameter. The process of reducing and lengthening wire with this tool is called drawing down.

Enameling: A process for coloring jewelry by fusing a special type of glass to the surface of the metal.

Engraving: A process of decorating metal by cutting away the surface with sharp tools called gravers.

Etching: The controlled corrosion of a metal surface with resists and acids to create a texture or pattern.

Fabrication: Construction of jewelry from sheet and wire using hand tools. It is the most demanding of jewelry-making processes due to its requirements of high skill training, material understanding, and tool knowledge.

Faceted: A gemstone cut of flat, highly polished planes at angles to one another that reflect light.

Findings/Fittings: Elements that contribute to the wearability of a piece of jewelry. Findings are usually machine made, and fittings are handmade catches, pin stems, ear-wires, and bails.

Finish: The final surface treatment on a piece and the quality of craftsmanship on the overall piece.

Firescale: A subsurface discoloration of oxidized copper on sterling silver that has been heated too long or too hot without a protective flux.

Flask: a steel cylinder used to hold a wax model and investment during the lost-wax casting process.

Flex-shaft: A versatile jewelry tool consisting of a precision high-speed motor, a flexible extension to a hand piece, and a foot rheostat. It is used for drilling, grinding, sanding, carving, and polishing jewelry.

Flux: A chemical used to coat the surface of metals during soldering to protect against the formation of oxides.

Forging: The process of shaping metal primarily through hammering.

Fusing: A technique of joining metals by melting them together.

Gemstones: Precious and semiprecious stones used in jewelry.

Gold: A precious, naturally yellow metal traditionally used to make jewelry. Extremely soft in its purest state, gold is alloyed to silver and copper to create different tones and make it tougher.

Graver: A sharp steel tool used for engraving and stone setting.

Hinge: A movable joint that turns or swings in a single plane, used to articulate two parts.

Ingot: A massive unit of metal, typically cast as the first step before milling out wire or sheet in a more usable size.

Inlay: A process by which one metal is fused or soldered into a recess in another metal. The surface is then filed flush, so that the recessed material becomes clearly defined.

Investment: In jewelry, it refers to the plaster used to make molds in lost-wax casting.

Karat: A proportional unit used to describe the purity of gold. Since 24k is pure gold, 14k is 14 parts of pure gold to 10 parts alloy.

Kiln: A small insulated oven capable of reaching high temperatures.

Layout: The process of determining, measuring, and marking out the elements and parts that will go into a piece of jewelry.

Liver of Sulfur: Potassium sulfide mixed with water to make a solution that will blacken copper and silver.

Lost-Wax Casting: A process in which a wax replica is encased in plaster, after which the plaster flask is heated in a kiln to the point where the wax is burnt out, leaving a cavity into which molten metal is poured. The plaster mold must then be destroyed to recover the casting.

Mallet: A hammer-shaped tool made of a material, such as rubber, leather, horn, and wood, that will not seriously mark the metal.

Mandrel: A tapered shaft, usually steel, around which metal is pressed or hammered to change its shape. Examples include ring mandrels, bracelet mandrels, and bezel mandrels.

Mokume Gane: A process in which layers of metal are fused together, creating a mokume laminate. The layers are then exposed through etching, filing, and milling.

Patina: A color coating on metal that can occur naturally or through the application of chemicals.

Peen: The end of a hammerhead opposite the face, typically wedge-shaped, curved, or spherical. To peen is to strike the metal.

Pickle: An acidic solution, such as sulfuric acid, used to clean metal.

Piercing: A process of creating negative space in a design by drilling holes, threading a saw blade through the hole, and sawing to remove material from the inside of a shape.

Plating: A fine coating of metal deposited on a metallic surface by means of an electric current.

Platinum: A precious metal that is a darker gray than silver and approximately twice as dense.

Polish: Metal finish that involves cleaning the piece of unwanted blemishes, rough spots, and uneven edges or surfaces.

Punches: Hardened steel tools used to decorate, texture, or form metal.

Raising: Forcing metal into three-dimensional forms through the use of hammers and stakes.

Repoussé: An ancient process in which sheet metal is hammered into contours from the front and the back.

Reticulation: A heat-based process that creates a rich, random surface texture through the use of discrepancies in the shrinkage rates of the alloys in a metal.

Rivet: A pin used to mechanically join components without heat or solder. The ends of the pin are spread to keep the parts from coming apart.

Roll Printing: A technique in which a rolling mill is used to imprint textures and patterns on sheet metal under pressure.

Rolling Mill: A piece of equipment consisting of two parallel, hardened steel cylinders mounted in a sturdy frame, used to reduce the size of sheet stock or wire.

Silver: An elemental metal of light-gray color known for its purity, malleability, and bright shine. Since pure silver is soft, it is alloyed to (75 parts per thousand) copper to create sterling silver (stamped 925).

Solder: An alloy of specific melting temperature and surface tension used to join metals. The process is called soldering.

Sprue: A wax or metal attachment to a wax model or metal master, which creates a funnel for pouring molten metal into a casting flask or for injecting molten wax into a rubber mold.

Stamping: The technique of impressing shapes and textures onto metal surfaces through the use of hardened steel tools called punches.

Steel: An alloy of iron and carbon.

Tabs: Cold connections in which fingers or strips of metal are bent over an element to secure it in place.

Temper: The hardness or toughness of a metal as produced by working, milling, thermally treating, or annealing the metal to a specified, consistent state. For most jewelry manufacture, the three states of dead-soft, half-hard, full work-hardened are important to know.

Texture: A visual or tactile surface given to a form.

Upset: To flare the end of a rivet by pounding the metal down on itself.

Work Hardening: The characteristic of metals to become tough and brittle when undergoing forces such as hammering, drawing, bending, rolling, and compressing.

Index

Aalund, Nanz, 10, 11, 120, 189-195, 196-200, 208
Acetylene, 112, 113
Advantages of apprenticeship, 13, 14
Air-fuel torch, 110, 111, 119
Apprentice Competency Framework, 49, 57-59, 126
Apprentice profile, 27
Assessment of apprentice's performance, 55
BEaJEWELER program, 28, 195
Behavioral Based Interviewing, 29-30
Bending/shaping tools, 67, 71-78, 84
Buffing safety, 87, 93-94, 95, 97-98, 118
Casting safety, 87, 90-92
Chamber of Commerce, U.S., 28
College credits for apprentice, 19
Compensation for apprentice, 18
Coryell, Ronda, 185-187
Cutting tools, 67, 68-70, 84
Dawson, Gary, 19, 22-25
Degree programs (college/university/technical school), 7, 194-195
Drill press safety, 87, 99-103, 118
Fair Labor Standard Act, 18

Ganoksin Project, 28, 191, 192
Gemological Institute of America (GIA), 28
Green, Timothy, 34, 35-37
Grinding safety, 87, 94-98, 118
Grouping, 46, 47-52, 150
   Fabricating and finishing skill set, 48-49
   Lost-wax casting skill set, 51
   Milling and draw plate usage skill set, 51-52
   Pouring ingots skill set, 50-51
   Sawing and filing skill set, 47-48
Haemer, Jo G., 32-34, 37
Hydraulic press safety, 87, 104-107, 119
Hydrogen, 112, 113
Internship program, 19, 22-25, 28
Interviewing (of apprentice candidates), 29-31
Jewelers of America Master Bench Jeweler certification, 186, 194, 195
Laser welding safety, 87, 108-109
Learning objectives, 6, 41, 42, 43-45, 46, 52, 54, 55, 56
Legal regulations for establishing apprenticeship, 16, 18, 20
Liquefied petroleum gas, 112
Manual dexterity tests, 30

Measuring/marking tools, 67, 79-81, 85
Methane, 110, 113
MJSA, 11, 28
Natural gas, 110, 111, 113
Non-compete agreement, 20, 42
Oxy-fuel torch, 110, 111, 119
Patania, Sam, 129, 131, 173, 175, 182-185
Poirier, G. Phil, 60-62, 64, 65
Propane, 110, 112, 113, 119
Projects (step by step)
　Filing cuff bracelets, 128-137
　Introductory filigree bead, 174-181
　Rivet capture pendant, 148-159
　Slot-in-slot construction, 160-173
　Soldering exercises, 125-127
　Wax carving, 138-147
Rotary (business organization), 28
Safety
　Buffing and grinding, 93-98
　Casting, 90-92
　Drill presses, 99-103
　General rules for apprentice, 88-89
　Hydraulic press, 104-107
　Laser equipment, 108-109
　Precautions (before hiring apprentice), 16
　Torch procedures, 110-117
Safety tests
　Buffing machine/grinding wheel, 97-98
　Drill presses, 97
　General rules, 89
　Hydraulic press, 107

Torch Work, 116-117
Samora, Maria, 61, 63-65
Scaffolding, 46, 53
Security precautions (prior to apprenticeship), 16
Self-directed learning, 6, 191, 192,
Small Business Administration (SBA), 16
SMART training objectives, 44, 46, 52
Supervisor, appointment of, 15
Support tasks for apprentice (list), 40
Technical schools, 194-195
Time frames for apprenticeships
　90-day apprenticeship model, 41
　Six-month apprenticeship model, 42
　Two-year apprenticeship model, 42
Tools (by groups)
　Cutting, 68-70, 84
　Bending/shaping, 71-78, 84
　Measuring/marking, 79-81, 85
　Torch, 82-83, 85
Torch
　gases, 110
　safety, 110-117
　tools, 82, 110
Women's Jewelry Association (WJA), 28
Worley, Amber, 120-122

About the Author

Nanz Aalund is an educator and award-winning jewelry artist based in Poulsbo, Washington. After serving an apprenticeship at a jewelry store outside Chicago (near where she grew up), she earned a BFA at Northern Illinois University and, later, an MFA in metals at the University of Washington, studying under renowned jeweler Mary Lee Hu. Nanz's wide-ranging career has included teaching jewelry and metals classes at the University of Washington and at the Art Institute of Seattle; designing and consulting for Nordstrom, Rudolf Erdel, Neiman Marcus, and Tiffany & Co., among others; serving as associate editor for *Art Jewelry* magazine; and creating her own series of instructional DVDs on jewelry-making techniques. Throughout it all, she has pursued a course of continuous learning, and her studies in jewelry design and manufacturing have taken her to Berlin, Paris, London, Florence, San Francisco, and New York.

About the Consulting Editor

Master goldsmith **Charles Lewton-Brain** is an associate professor and the former head of the jewelry and metals program at the Alberta College of Art and Design in Alberta, Canada. Educated in Germany, Canada, and the United States, he has written extensively on jewelry-making techniques (including foldforming, a revolutionary method he invented for manipulating sheet metal). His honors include the Saidye Bronfman Award, Canada's highest prize for craft.